FRENCH CLASSICS

EASY AND ELEVATED DISHES

TO COOK AT HOME

Matthew Ryle

BLOOMSBURY PUBLISHING

NEW YORK • LONDON • OXFORD • NEW DELHI • SYDNEY

This book is for my wonderful wife Rachel
and our beautiful baby boy Alfie.

FRENCH CLASSICS

EASY AND ELEVATED DISHES
TO COOK AT HOME

Matthew Ryle

CONTENTS

—•—

Foreword

Dear Matt,

What an achievement! With deep love and passion for the humble home-cooked dishes of France, as well as for bistro and brasserie classics, you have created a beautiful debut cookbook that is filled with mouth-watering recipes and stunning photographs. I absolutely love it.

Within these pages you have served up a true feast, just as you do at Maison François, where I have sat at lunchtimes with my friends and loved ones, merrily drinking a sumptuous, powerful, punchy Gigondas while relishing the food: a well-risen cheese soufflé; globe artichokes with sauce ravigote; roast chicken with frites; steak au poivre... Slowly the meal leads towards cheeses and the dessert trolley, a triumphant showcase-on-wheels for irresistible classics such as Paris-Brest, crème caramel and crème brûlée. I am salivating at the memories.

So many dishes in this book evoke the fondest recollections of my beloved Maman Blanc at the chopping board, the hob or the oven door, or carrying vast platters to the table. Every plate and bowl would be licked clean by my siblings and me. From white asparagus with beurre blanc, to celeriac rémoulade, tartiflette and quiche Lorraine, to sole meunière, boeuf bourguignon and coq au vin; they are all here in this book. You include a recipe for French onion soup, which, as a teenager, I would rustle up for my friends after a night on the town. I am not sure if your chocolate mousse can beat Maman's, but I'll certainly try it and let you know...

You have also covered the specialities of home cooking in Provence and the south of France, which I first visited at about the age of twelve and, again, your fantastic recipes spark early food memories of pistou soup and ratatouille, as well as bouillabaisse, that fantastic fish soup, which I adore with a dollop of rouille and garlic-rubbed croutons. At sweet-scented boulangeries I tried pissaladière, not quite a pizza, but similar and topped with lightly caramelised onions, criss-crossed with anchovies and dotted with black olives. Often these dishes require little skill to make, but they do need good-quality ingredients, a bit of patience, some passion and – if you are a cook at home – plenty of affection for those who will be eating the food that you make.

Matt, you have told me how, as a young boy, you would watch me as I cooked on television. This, you say, partly inspired your decision to become a chef. My own childhood was spent foraging for mushrooms and hunting for asparagus in the dark and mysterious forests of Franche-Comté. But I must tell you that I am extremely glad that you were glued to a television screen. All of us who come to Maison François – and the readers of this book – have certainly benefitted from your childhood viewing and I feel humbled.

You are truly carrying the torch of French cookery for the next generation, and I am extremely proud that you came to Le Manoir as a young apprentice and spent time training in our kitchens. I am delighted to be here with you and send to you – the chef – my compliments, as well as my heartiest congratulations.

Vive la France et bon appétit!

Raymond Blanc

Raymond Blanc OBE

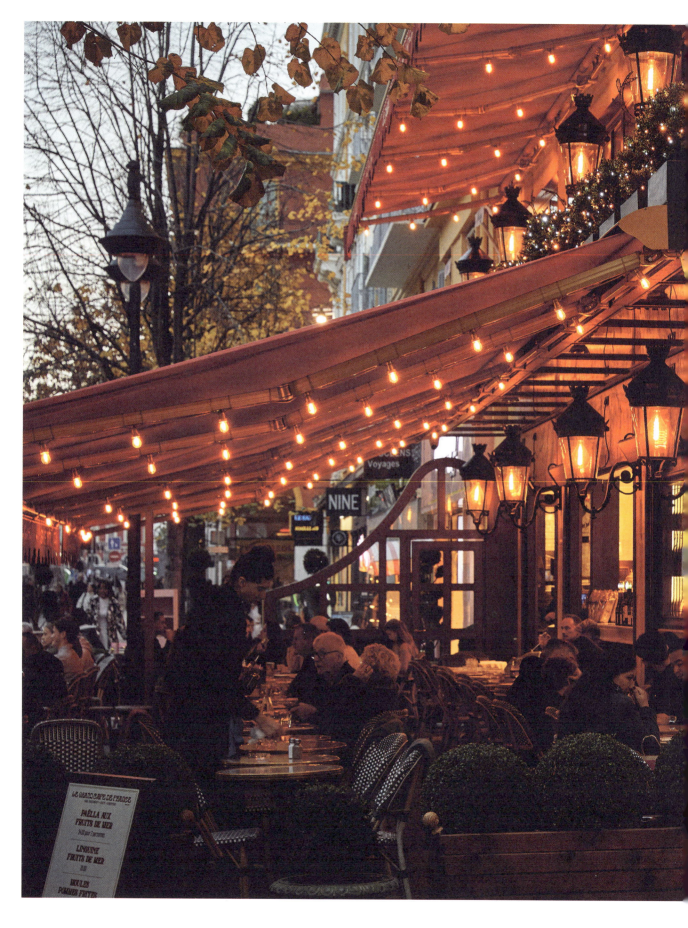

Introduction

I suppose I should start by explaining how my deeply rooted love of French food came about. To do that, we need to go back a little bit. Being born in the French countryside and taught to cook from the land at a young age by my grandfather (himself a chef for more than forty years) would have been an ideal start... Unfortunately, my beginnings were a lot closer to home, in a village called Purley on Thames, close to far-from-glamorous Reading.

Whether or not I knew it at the time, my obsession with French food started at an early age. The simple pleasure of slurping pots of supermarket crème caramel as a kid remains vivid in my head. That first bite of a croque madame on a family ski trip to the French Alps, like no other ham and cheese toastie I had ever experienced. And though my initial encounter with French onion soup on that same holiday caused some battle wounds in the form of a burnt tongue, every time I catch its scent – simmering on the stove or wafting through a restaurant – I'm transported to a place of scalding happiness. However, ultimately it was as a food-fixated teenager in a French-focused chef school, cooking these dishes for the very first time, that my passion was really ignited.

This is a cookbook not only about my favourite recipes, food memories and experiences, but also about how French cookery has shaped who I am.

French food is your friend. If you need a hug after a long hard day at work, open this book and cook your problems away. It's the ultimate home cooking. This food is for everyone: it's about cooking and eating with friends and family, not about fancy restaurant plates. I wanted to create a book that you can use on any weeknight to create a tasty dinner, and also that offers something special for when the in-laws are coming over and you hope to impress them.

This is my favourite food to eat. Roast chicken, a plate of chips piled high and a salad of crisp lettuce with a simple vinaigrette. Melting beef, chewy lardons and a rich, velvety red wine sauce. A simple bowl of mussels steamed with white wine, garlic and parsley. A perfect meal for me and many others consists of dishes such as these, almost universally appealing and forever satisfying to eat, yet most of us don't cook them at home. It's time to change that!

I flew the nest, aged sixteen, in pursuit of French food. I embarked on a specialised chef's scholarship where basic stocks, the 'mother sauces', cutting techniques and French regional specialities were all on the curriculum. I was fascinated by the history of food in France; finally it all made sense. French cooks worked with what they had to hand: this is how the classic dishes were born. Coq au vin was created when the world-famous poultry from Bresse met red wine from Burgundy. Dairy and cheese production in the Savoie? Welcome, tartiflette. There is an explanation like this for every single one of the canonical dishes. They aren't about special ingredients; indeed, the French classics typically use relatively common and inexpensive produce. Often, all that's needed to elevate them to exquisite heights is allowing time and the cooking process to work their magic.

I won't bore you with a list of restaurants I have worked at, but in the past fifteen-plus years I have been fortunate enough to cook with some of the best chefs and mentors in the world. The short period I spent with Raymond Blanc at Le Manoir opened my eyes to the joys of French food the most. It's enough to say that, over my career, I've learned a huge range of techniques in high-end kitchens. Now, I run two busy, bustling brasseries in central London – Maison François and Café François – but it's the simple methods and recipes from my college days that remain the tools I rely on most. And in the pages that follow, I'll be passing all of them on to you.

This book is full of French dishes that have stood the test of time, most of them straightforward, others needing a little more time or skill, but all of them set out clearly and including tips, pointers and essentials picked up over my many years of cooking them professionally. Sure, I'm a chef, but my whole approach is about explaining methods simply, understanding what home cooks want. Whether you prefer to serve your coq au vin with microwave rice or decadent *pommes purée* is up to you; it's your choice if you follow my recipe for homemade stock when cooking chicken and mushroom fricassée or simply use a shop-bought version (though I'll try to convince you why making your own is worth it). This book isn't about making life harder than it need be, I just want you to enjoy cooking this delicious food as much as I do!

I started sharing my love of French food on social media, making recipe videos for traditional dishes, and I've been blown away by the response. My aim was to remind people of dishes they once loved but have forgotten, to give mouth-watering recipes, put classic French food back on the agenda and show that this kind of cooking is easier than people think. French food has earned an unfair reputation for being complicated to make and I want to dispel that notion.

Let's take the example of one of France's most famous dishes: boeuf bourguignon. A rich stew originating from Burgundy (renowned for its excellent wine and prized Charolais cattle), this is a dish – like so many of the classics – that started as a peasant recipe, a means to slow-cook tough, unwanted cuts of meat using the ingredients to hand. Then, in 1903, chef Auguste Escoffier published a version of the recipe that refined it into the haute cuisine dish which it is generally regarded as today, despite its humble home-cooking roots. Sure, it takes a while to make (with both long marinating and cooking times), but really, it's very simple to execute well with minimal effort. If it was chefs who made this simple everyday food into haute cuisine, it's only fair that another chef brings the recipes back to their domestic beginnings.

Writing a book about French classic dishes is intimidating; the people of France are very protective of their food, and rightly so. So I'll tell you upfront that, while these are as true to the original recipes – as I know them – as they can be, some have been slightly adapted for ease in a present-day kitchen. These are *my* French classics: we live busy lives and this book is a modern approach to making these timeless dishes accessible. I want my recipes to help you to become a better cook. I've included the dishes that have given me my culinary scars, those I got wrong a hundred times and more. But now, after years of trial and error, I have written every recipe in this book with the thought in the front of my mind of my mum – a great home cook, but quite set in her repertoire – being able to pick it up and cook from it without any issues at all. Hopefully this book will help you (and my mum) push the boundaries and jazz things up... I'm sure my dad would be happy if his weeknight meals were to get a *French Classics* facelift.

Each recipe falls into the category of either 'EASY' or 'ELEVATED', marked at the top of the ingredients list, helping you to choose which dishes to make on any given occasion. Start with the basics and work your way up to more complex dishes; that's how I did it when learning how to cook. Each recipe has specific tips for success, but there is one bit of kit I always recommend: get yourself an accurate digital probe thermometer. In this book, I use it on multiple occasions; it'll help simplify things in the kitchen, make you a more confident cook, and – without doubt – will be the best money (and not much of it) that you'll ever spend on equipment; it takes all the guesswork out of cooking.

I wrote this book with my first child on the way, and, now that it's published and in your hands, my amazing wife and I have an eight-month-old baby, so at least the book-writing happened with a clear head and plenty of sleep! Where am I going with this thought? It's that, one day, I hope to cook and share the recipes in these pages with my little family, making memories for life, and I want you to do the same in your kitchen for the people you love the most, too. Don't be afraid of failure; even if something doesn't quite go to plan, it's all part of the memories.

This is food made for big tables, for sharing. And ultimately, it's this sense of connection that makes us treasure French cookery: it's food that makes you happy. In recent years, we've seen a real renaissance in French cuisine as part of the restaurant scene and now it's time to start enjoying it at home again, too. This is *the* food of the moment and for very good reason: with these recipes, you're always in for a good meal: wholesome, heart-warming and satisfying.

La grande fête

Yes, all the classic recipes in France have humble home-cooking roots and, yes, this book contains dishes you can cook on any weeknight. But it also offers something special for when you want to put on *la grande fête* ('the big feast'). So I wanted to make a few suggestions for your next celebration, for whatever time of year that might fall. Here, I've put together my perfect sharing feasts for each season. So, whether the sun is shining and you're eating outdoors, or cold winds are blowing and you're cosy by the fire, invite your friends over, open a few bottles of something and let the good times roll.

A three-course meal can be quite an undertaking, so look at my tips with each recipe – they are the passages in italics – to help you get organised and make things a bit easier.

———•———

SPRING

Soupe au Pistou (see page 26)

~

Lamb Shoulder, Pommes Boulangère
(see page 140)

Green Asparagus, Sauce Gribiche
(see page 209)

Spring Cabbage, Anchoïade, Chilli
(see page 212)

~

Crème Caramel (see page 234)

SUMMER

Shellfish Cocktail (see page 44)

~

Dijon Roast Chicken (see page 128)

Ratatouille, Sauce Pistou
(see page 193)

Tomato Salad, Vierge Dressing
(see page 208)

~

Raspberry Soufflé (see page 224)

AUTUMN

Country Terrine (see page 54)

Celeriac Rémoulade (see page 33)

~

Lobster Thermidor (see page 102)

Pommes Pont Neuf (see page 172)

Green Salad (see page 197)

~

Cherry and Almond Clafoutis
(see page 229)

WINTER

French Onion Soup (see page 22)

~

Beef Bourguignon (see page 154)

Pommes Purée (see page 179)

Chicory Salad, Capers, Parsley
(see page 196)

~

Tarte Tatin (see page 246)

STARTERS

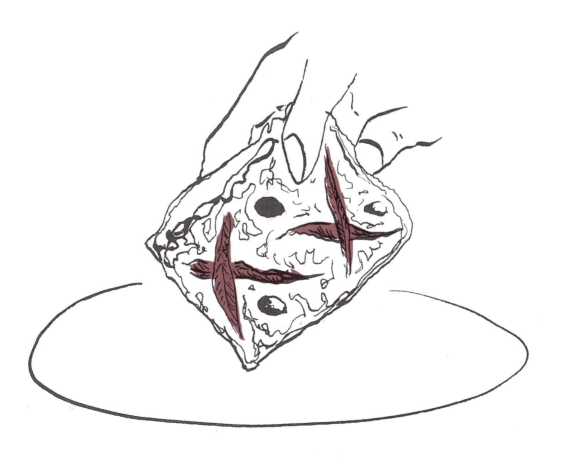

Le grand aïoli

A sharing starter dish from Provence, think of this as a summery answer to the more autumnal charcuterie board. The star of the elegant platter is aïoli, a deliciously thick garlicky sauce that is a staple in my fridge. Once you've tried it, you'll be searching for excuses to dip everything into this magnificent mayonnaise. Traditionally, the aïoli is surrounded by all sorts of fresh 'dippables': crisp seasonal vegetables, halved eggs, poached salt cod (left out here for ease) and crusty bread. It is a healthy way to kick off the perfect spring/summer meal, and, artfully displayed, vibrant vegetables make any table look great.

————— • —————

This platter doesn't need to be a fancy affair, as a pared-down version works equally well, so serve it with whatever you want. Simple carrot, celery or cucumber batons will make for the perfect casual family plate, for instance. Treat making the aïoli as you would a mayonnaise: add the oil very slowly, especially at first. When adding the oil, the sauce will get very thick, so use the lemon juice and perhaps a splash of water to loosen it as you go, allowing you to continue pouring in the total amount of oil.

EASY

~

Prep time 20 minutes

Serves 4 as a sharing starter

~

For the aïoli

2 egg yolks

20ml (4 tsp) white wine vinegar

10g (2 tsp) Dijon mustard

1 garlic clove, finely grated

10g (2 tsp) Confit Garlic (see page 254, about 2 cloves)

340ml (generous 1⅓ cups) rapeseed oil, or other good-quality vegetable oil

10ml (2 tsp) lemon juice

Sea salt flakes and fresh-cracked black pepper

To serve

Selection of seasonal vegetables: radishes (with perky green leaves, if possible), Baby Gem lettuces, fennel bulbs, cooked green beans or sugar snaps, carrots, cucumber (pick as many or as few as you like)

4 eggs, boiled for 8 minutes (see page 82)

8 good-quality anchovy fillets

1. This aïoli recipe makes slightly more than you need for 4 people, but you'll thank me later when you're dipping your chips into it. Put the egg yolks, white wine vinegar, mustard, grated garlic clove and confit garlic into a blender and, while blending, *very* slowly stream in the oil – going especially slowly at first – adding a little of the lemon juice when the aïoli gets too thick. When you're out of lemon juice, continue adding oil, and, if it gets too thick again, splash in just a little water. Carry on until you have used all the oil. You should be left with a nice thick aïoli. Check and adjust the seasoning, then spoon into a serving bowl.

2. Cut your chosen vegetables into manageable, attractive pieces. Get a large sharing platter and arrange your vegetables on it nicely.

3. Cut your eggs in half, put them among the vegetables and drape an anchovy fillet over each half. Serve your generous bowl of aïoli in the centre.

French onion soup

I remember the first time I ate this: I was a young boy stopping for a family lunch on my first ski trip to the Alps, when out came a bubbling cauldron of onions, cheese and bread. My mum warned me it would be hot, but, as I'm sure is the case with most people, I found the aroma too tempting and burned my tongue, as I've done nearly every time since. A staple in restaurants across France, the recipe actually originated as a humble peasant soup made with just onions, stale bread and water. Today's version might be a bit fancier, but this is still wonderfully simple to make at home. Slowly caramelised onions melting into a rich beef broth, slowly absorbed by day-old baguette covered in molten Gruyère cheese... the ultimate comfort food, my perfect lunch with a simple Green Salad (see page 197).

———— • ————

The secret ingredient to this soup is time, as the onions need to be cooked very low and slow. The more caramelised, deeper colour the onions develop, the more flavour they'll have. Although making your own stock will result in the most authentic-tasting soup, shop-bought stock will do the trick so long as your onions have received enough love. It's not traditional, but my other secret is a splash of soy sauce, which adds richness and makes those caramelised onion flavours sing.

EASY

~

Prep time 15 minutes
Cooking time 70–80 minutes
Serves 4 as a starter or light meal

~

* You will need 4 ovenproof soup bowls that can go under a grill.

1.5kg (3lb 5oz) onions (about 6), finely sliced

100g (7 tbsp) butter

3 garlic cloves, crushed

3 bay leaves

Leaves from a few thyme sprigs

300ml (1¼ cups) white wine

1.3 litres (5½ cups) good-quality beef stock (for homemade, see page 267)

50ml (3½ tbsp) soy sauce

½ baguette, 1 day old

250g (2½ cups grated) Gruyère cheese

Sea salt flakes and fresh-cracked black pepper

1. Slowly caramelise the onions in the butter in a wide, heavy-based pan. After 10 minutes, add a pinch of salt, the garlic and bay leaves. Cook, stirring regularly, until the onions are caramelised and brown, about 45 minutes. I know this sounds a long time, but it's worth it.

2. Add the thyme to the onions, along with the wine. Bring to a simmer and cook until the wine has reduced by half.

3. Add the beef stock and soy sauce and gently simmer for around 10 minutes. Meanwhile, cut the baguette into 2cm- (¾in-) thick slices and grate the Gruyère cheese.

4. Preheat the grill. Check the seasoning of the soup, adding salt and pepper if required. Ladle the hot soup into 4 ovenproof bowls that can go under the grill, top with the baguette slices and mound high with grated Gruyère, dividing it evenly between the bowls. Place under the hot grill until golden brown and bubbling, then serve.

Cervelle de canut

I only came across this delicious cheese and herb dish relatively recently, about five years ago. I was writing the first menus for Maison François and struggling for vegetarian starters, as those were remaining stubbornly pork- and duck-heavy. I did some research, stumbled across this dish and made it. It's reminiscent of sour cream and chive dip, but on steroids... I love it! It is a speciality of Lyon, somewhere between a dip and cheese spread. The dish's base is fromage blanc (a fresh, mild cheese similar to ricotta or cottage cheese) mixed with Brillat-Savarin, crème fraîche, herbs, shallots, mustard, vinegar and seasoning. In Lyon, it is served as a perfect summer starter, with fresh or toasted baguette.

———— • ————

This is fantastic spread over crusty bread, yes, but it can be enjoyed in so many other ways, so my advice is to get creative with it. Pair it with crunchy radishes, use it as a topping for loaded jacket potatoes or skins, as a dip for a packet of salted crisps, or – if you're feeling fancy – use it instead of the soft cheese you usually have in a cucumber or smoked salmon sandwich. The possibilities are endless, and, once you've thrown together this simple dip once, it'll become a staple in your weekly routine.

EASY

~

Prep time 10 minutes
Serves 4 as a starter

~

75g (5 tbsp) Brillat-Savarin cheese, weighed without the white rind

100g (7 tbsp) fromage blanc, ideally, or cream cheese if you can't find it

100g (7 tbsp) crème fraîche

5ml (1 tsp) good-quality white wine vinegar, ideally Chardonnay

40g (¼ cup) finely chopped shallot (about 1 large or 2 medium-small)

1 tsp chopped chives

1 tsp chopped chervil, or chopped parsley leaves

1 tsp chopped tarragon leaves

Finely grated zest of ½ lemon

15g (1 tbsp) Dijon mustard

Sea salt flakes and fresh-cracked black pepper

1. Put the Brillat-Savarin into a bowl and, using a spoon, beat the cheese until it has a smooth consistency. Next, add the fromage blanc or cream cheese and crème fraîche and mix well, again until smooth.

2. Finish the cervelle by adding all the remaining ingredients, check the seasoning and add more salt and pepper if required. This will sit happily in the fridge, covered, for up to 5 days, while you spoon it over everything.

Soupe au pistou

More glorious Provençal cuisine! This comforting dish is almost a complete meal in itself, a traditional southern French soup made using an array of summer vegetables, such as tomatoes, courgettes and green beans. But, for me, what makes it so irresistible is the garlicky dollop of herby *pistou* on top. *Pistou* is Frances's answer to pesto, made by pounding basil, garlic, lemon and olive oil together.

———— • ————

This is a summer dish, but I make it all year and it's equally delicious. Just substitute the vegetables with whatever is bang in season. Pistou *will sit happily in the fridge for a few days, but if you're feeling lazy, as I often am, store-bought pesto will do the trick.* Soupe au pistou *is the French cousin to minestrone, so a dollop of pesto – while not traditional – seems pretty fitting. Don't worry, I won't tell...*

EASY

~

Prep time 20 minutes
Cooking time 40 minutes
Serves 4 as a starter or light meal

~

For the pistou

50g (2oz) bunch of basil, leaves picked

70ml (scant 5 tbsp) olive oil

Finely grated zest and juice of ½ lemon

2 garlic cloves

Sea salt flakes and fresh-cracked black pepper

For the soup

1 carrot

2 celery sticks

1 onion

1 leek

2 courgettes

2 tomatoes

80g (¾ cup, cut) green beans

50ml (generous 3 tbsp) olive oil, plus more to serve

2 garlic cloves, finely chopped

2 bay leaves

80g (⅔ cup) peas

100g (½ cup) cooked butter beans

Parmesan cheese, to serve

1. Place a saucepan of water on the stove to boil. To make sure your *pistou* stays green, we are going to blanch the basil leaves, so have a small bowl of iced water ready too. Place the picked leaves in the boiling water for 10 seconds, then, using a slotted spoon, remove the basil and put it into the iced water to stop the cooking. Remove the basil and squeeze out the excess water, then place in a blender with the olive oil, lemon zest and juice, garlic and seasoning and blend until smooth. Pulse-blend a few times to mix, then check the seasoning and set aside. This will sit happily in the fridge for 5 days, but also freezes well.

2. Chop the carrot, celery, onion, leek, courgettes and tomatoes into roughly 1cm (½ inch) pieces. Cut the green beans into 2cm (¾ inch) lengths. Place a wide-based saucepan over a medium-low heat, add the oil and leave for a minute to heat up. Add the carrot, celery, onion, leek, garlic and bay leaves and cook slowly until completely soft, but without colour. Cover with 1 litre (1 quart) water, bring to the boil and simmer for around 15 minutes.

3. Now add the courgettes, tomatoes and green beans and cook for another 5 minutes. Add the peas and butter beans and simmer for 2 minutes before adding the *pistou* to finish, if you want to stir it through the soup, keeping back 4 dollops to serve. As soon as you have stirred the *pistou* through the soup, stop the cooking and serve up.

4. Ladle into warmed bowls, add a spoon of *pistou* to each, drizzle with olive oil and top with grated Parmesan, serving any remaining *pistou* on the side.

Comté gougères

ELEVATED

~

**Prep time 15 minutes, plus cooling
(if needed) and resting**

Cooking time 25 minutes

Makes 10

~

* You will need a piping bag.

50g (3 tbsp) butter

½ tsp sea salt flakes

100ml (7 tbsp) water

100ml (7 tbsp) whole milk

125g (1 cup) plain flour

60g (⅔ cup) Parmesan cheese,
finely grated

85g (¾ cup) Comté cheese, finely
grated, plus more to serve

4 eggs, plus more if needed

A *gougère* is a savoury choux pastry puff – think cheesy profiterole – baked into a crisp, airy pocket of delight. My favourite cheese to use is Comté, but feel free to swap this out for your preferred hard cheese, anything from Gruyère to Cheddar will work well. This is a wonderful make-ahead recipe: simply stash them in the freezer, ready to bake whenever you get a *gougère* craving. We serve more than 50,000 of these every year at the restaurant, so I've become something of an expert on preparing them. A great snack at any time and heavenly while sipping on a cold glass of wine or Champagne.

Best eaten straight from the oven, *gougères* should always be served warm and covered in grated cheese. I like to make them whenever I have friends over for drinks, as there's something special about the room filling up with that baked cheese smell while you're handing out warm *gougères*. It makes you feel like Nigella.

———— • ————

This choux base is quick and easy to whip up. Temperature is important when preparing your choux: you need the mix to be hot enough to melt the cheese in the first instance, but leave it to cool slightly before adding the eggs, as you don't want those to scramble. Sometimes, after adding the eggs, the mix is still too firm to pipe – most often if your eggs were on the smaller side – so make sure you have a few extra eggs around in case they're needed to correct the consistency. At all costs, do not open the oven while baking, as this will cause your cheese puffs to, well, lose their puff!

If you're filling the freezer, you can pipe the gougères on to a small tray, side by side. Once they are frozen solid, you can break them apart and store in a freezer bag. When it comes to baking, follow the same steps as in the recipe, leaving the same gap between each as you lay them out on the baking tray.

1. Chop the butter into small pieces and put in a saucepan with the salt, measured water and milk. Place over a high heat and bring to the boil. Once the butter has melted and everything is bubbling away, reduce the temperature to low, add the flour and cook for around 5 minutes, continually stirring with a spatula.

2. Pour the cooked mixture into a stand mixer fitted with a paddle attachment, if you have one. If not, a bowl, spatula and some elbow grease will work. Add both grated cheeses and mix on a medium speed until the cheese has melted and the mixture is combined. At this stage, the mix should be cool enough to start adding the eggs, but if it is visibly steaming, or hot to the touch, leave it for 5 minutes more to cool down.

3. Add the eggs 1 at a time, while mixing on a low speed, waiting until each egg is fully combined before adding the next. Once all 4 eggs are added, you should have a mixture that has a spooning consistency: take a spoon, scoop up the mix and tap the edge of the bowl to knock off the mix; it should come off with relative ease. If it is still a little too stiff, lightly beat another egg in a small bowl, then add it gradually until the consistency is perfect. Put the mix into a piping bag and leave to rest for 15–20 minutes.

4. Preheat the oven to 160°C fan (350°F).

5. On a baking tray lined with baking paper, pipe the *gougères*: you're aiming for something slightly bigger than a £2 coin (about 1 inch in diameter), leaving at least a 2cm (3/4 inch) gap between each. Wet the tip of your finger and tap down any peaks your piping has left.

6. Bake for 12 minutes without opening the oven door. When the timer runs out, turn the tray around and cook for a further 2–3 minutes until golden brown. Cover the hot *gougères* with finely grated Comté, then serve straight away.

Carottes râpées

Sibling to the celeriac *rémoulade* opposite, equally loved and just as delicious. Treat it in the same way, either as a great stand-alone dish, or as an accompaniment. You will find this everywhere in France: on bistro menus, sold pre-made in shops, on every deli display across the country. It is a very basic recipe that is quick to whip up on any day of the week: just grated carrots, herbs and a light mustard vinaigrette.

———— • ————

I like to pimp this vibrant salad with a sprinkling of dukkah, as spices such as cumin, fennel and coriander complement the carrots perfectly. Unlike the rémoulade *opposite, this salad is best made using a grater (*râpées *means 'grated'), because the vinaigrette here is thinner than the mayonnaise used for* rémoulade, *so grating the carrots helps everything to mix and bind together more effectively.*

EASY

~

Prep time 20 minutes

Cook time 6 minutes (optional, if making the dukkah)

Serves 4 as a starter or accompaniment

~

For the carrots

450g (1lb) carrots, peeled

40ml (2½ tbsp) olive oil

20ml (4 tsp) lemon juice, or more to taste

½ tsp sea salt flakes

10g (2 tsp) Dijon mustard

5g honey

5g (2 tsp) finely chopped herb leaves (parsley, tarragon, chives, chervil)

For the dukkah, to serve (optional)

120g (scant 1 cup) pumpkin seeds

120g (1 cup) sunflower seeds

5g dried thyme

4g fennel seeds

4g cumin seeds

3g coriander seeds

Sea salt flakes and fresh-cracked black pepper

1. Start with the dukkah, if you're making that. Preheat the oven to 180°C fan (400°F). Spread the pumpkin and sunflower seeds on a small baking tray and toast them in the oven for 4 minutes, then add all the other ingredients for the dukkah except the seasoning and toast for another 2 minutes.

2. Leave to cool, add some seasoning, then either chop with a very sharp knife (this is fiddly for beginners), lightly pulse-blend in a spice grinder, or smash in a mortar and pestle. You want a rubble rather than a smooth crumb, with some larger pieces or even whole seeds. Set aside.

3. Using a box grater, or a food processor fitted with the grater attachment, you want to grate the carrots down their length, so you end up with long pieces of grated carrot around 5cm (2 inches) long.

4. Put all the other ingredients for the carrots into a mixing bowl and whisk until emulsified. Add the grated carrots and some seasoning and mix well. Pile the carrots and their dressing high on a sharing platter, or plate smaller piles up individually. Sprinkle with dukkah, if you like, to serve: it is a nice touch, adding texture and interesting spice.

For a photograph, see page 83.

Celeriac rémoulade

Universally loved all around France and found everywhere, this all-time classic is made by tossing celeriac in a velvety mayonnaise-and-Dijon dressing, spiked with a little lemon juice for extra zing. Think of it as a coleslaw that actually tastes nice! Once I discovered it, I found myself putting it with everything: alongside roast chicken, in leftover beef sandwiches, or with a good piece of smoked salmon. It also makes a delicious starter in its own right, with some crunchy caper berries. Traditionally, it is served with charcuterie; try it with Country Terrine or a slice of *Pâté en Croûte* (see pages 54 and 46).

——— • ———

Many recipes call for the celeriac to be grated, but while that may be slightly easier, it results in a watery rémoulade *lacking in texture. I always recommend using a mandolin to cut the celeriac into thin sheets, then a knife to cut those into matchsticks (julienne). The texture and eating quality will be far superior, so the extra time spent will be appreciated. Be generous with your mustard dressing – you really can't overdo it – however, if there is any left, it will make a really beautiful chicken sandwich.*

EASY

~

Prep time 15 minutes
Serves 4–6 as a starter or accompaniment

~

* You will need a mandolin (optional, see tip, above).

Finely grated zest and juice of ½ lemon

50g (generous 3 tbsp) crème fraîche

125g (½ cup) mayonnaise (for homemade, see page 253)

25g (1 tbsp plus 2 tsp) wholegrain mustard

25g (1 tbsp plus 2 tsp) Dijon mustard

Pinch (½ tsp) of finely chopped parsley leaves

200g (about 2 cups julienned) celeriac (¼–½ medium celeriac, once trimmed)

Sea salt flakes and fresh-cracked black pepper

1. Put all the ingredients except the celeriac into a mixing bowl, mix well and set aside.

2. Peel the celeriac, if you have a sharp peeler, or if this isn't an option, cut the top and base off, then cut off the skin from the top to the bottom, trying to remove as little celeriac flesh as possible. Using a mandolin, if you have one, cut the celeriac into 1–2mm (1/12 inch) slices, then, using a knife, cut those into thin matchsticks, aka julienne. If you don't have a mandolin, both of these stages can be done with a knife.

3. Mix the celeriac into the dressing with some seasoning: I like to use my hands to make sure all the strands are evenly dressed. The *rémoulade* will now sit happily, covered and in the fridge, for a few hours before being eaten, so feel free to get it done in advance of your meal. When you're ready to eat, give it a last mix and finish with cracked black pepper on top.

For a photograph, see page 57.

Vichyssoise

Turns out my mum was knocking out French classics long before I was even a chef. Leek and potato soup was a regular occurrence in our house when I was growing up and it was one of my favourite things to eat on the weekend. Okay, my mum wasn't exactly making vichyssoise, as her version was served hot... but it's believed the chef who created this dish was actually inspired by his mother's hot leek and potato soup too, in his case from the town of Vichy in France. He made this chilled version as a way to cool off in the summer, and, though it's traditionally served cold, it is also great warmed up in the winter.

———— • ————

Don't worry, it's easier to make than it is to say. Vish-ee-swahz is a simple soup with a rich, creamy texture coming from the potatoes and a gentle sweetness from the leeks. Sweat the onion, shallots and leeks at a very low temperature for a long time to extract their maximum natural sweetness. And blend it for a full five minutes: the super-smooth, velvety texture is what makes vichyssoise *so special. I like to serve the finished soup with some croutons for texture and chives to point up the other three alliums, but you could add a dollop of crème fraîche, if you like.*

EASY

~

Prep time 20 minutes
Cooking time 30 minutes
Serves 4 as a starter or light meal

~

For the soup
150g (1 stick plus 2 tbsp) butter
1 onion, finely sliced
2 shallots, finely sliced
3 leeks, white parts only, finely sliced
3 garlic cloves, chopped
150g (1 cup) peeled and chopped potato (about ½ large)
2 bay leaves
50:50 whole milk and water, to cover
Sea salt flakes and fresh-cracked white pepper
Chopped chives, to serve

For the croutons
Stale sourdough bread
Olive oil

1. Put a wide-based pan over a medium-low heat and add the butter. When it has melted, sweat the onion, shallots, leeks and garlic until very soft, but with no colour, around 15 minutes. Add the remaining ingredients, season well and bring to the boil, then gently simmer for another 10–15 minutes or until the potatoes are completely soft.

2. Remove the bay leaves, then transfer the soup vegetables to a blender using a slotted spoon, leaving the liquid behind in the pan for now. Start blending, adding ladles of liquid until you get the correct consistency. (If you pour in everything directly from the pan, you might be left with a soup that is too thin.) Blend for 5 minutes until very smooth, then pour through a fine sieve into a clean saucepan or bowl. Check the seasoning and adjust it if needed, then leave to cool, if you want to eat this chilled.

3. Meanwhile, to make the croutons, preheat the oven to 160°C fan (350°F). Roughly chop some stale sourdough bread into croutons, dress with olive oil and bake on a baking tray until golden brown, around 6 minutes. Serve the soup – either chilled or gently reheated, as you prefer – scattered with the croutons and chives.

Pissaladière

Piss-a-lad-what?! When I was in my first year of training, each week my chef set me a new task: every time I was to learn about, then recreate, a classic French dish. *Pissaladière* was the first piece of homework I was set! Sweet caramelised onions, salty anchovies and olives make up the toppings for this classic Provençal dish. There are two options for the base: a yeasted dough similar to pizza, or puff pastry, which is my preferred choice and also easier to accomplish at home. My favourite way to enjoy this is at room temperature as part of a sunny picnic, with a glass of rosé if you're feeling boujee.

———— • ————

If you're looking to make your life as easy as possible, I would recommend cooking your onions in advance and embracing ready-rolled puff pastry. If you have both these components in the fridge, ready to go, this is a very simple recipe to make. The onions need to be cooked low and slow: the more caramelised, deeper colour they develop, the more flavour they'll have. Use the best-quality anchovies you can find and try to find a Niçoise olive for the most authentic-tasting pissaladière.

EASY

~

Prep time 15 minutes

Cooking time 45 minutes

Serves 4 as a light meal, or more as a starter or canapé / Makes 1 tart

~

4 onions, sliced

20ml (4 tsp) olive oil, plus more for the tray and to finish

320g sheet of shop-bought all-butter puff pastry (14-oz sheet all-butter puff pastry, thawed if frozen)

25 good-quality anchovy fillets

25 black olives, ideally Niçoise

Leaves from 4 thyme sprigs

Sea salt flakes and fresh-cracked black pepper

1. Put the sliced onions and olive oil in a wide pan, which has a lid, over a medium heat. Cover with the lid and allow to steam-fry for around 5 minutes. Add a pinch of salt and remove the lid to allow the liquid to evaporate, then continue to cook slowly, stirring frequently, until you have a dark caramelised mass. You want the onions to stick slightly, as scraping them from the bottom of the pan is what allows them to achieve that deep brown colour.

2. Preheat the oven to 220°C fan (475°F). Rub a baking tray with some olive oil and place your sheet of puff pastry on top. Top with the caramelised onions and spread nearly to the edges, leaving just a small section of visible crust. Bake for 15–20 minutes. The crust should puff and take on a nice colour and the underside should also be crisp.

3. Decorate the baked tart with your anchovies, olives and thyme, then finish with some olive oil and cracked black pepper. Traditionally, the anchovies form a lattice pattern, with the olives in the middle of each diamond. Cut into pieces and enjoy it while it's still warm!

Salade niçoise

Light enough to eat on a hot day, but hearty enough to stand in for dinner, a niçoise salad is a classic for good reason. This wonderful dish – which, it won't surprise you, hails from Nice – is made up (contrary to popular belief) of ripe tomatoes, cucumber, hard-boiled eggs, Niçoise olives, anchovies and canned tuna, then finished with good-quality olive oil, seasoning and basil leaves. The version containing green beans, potatoes, fresh seared tuna and vinaigrette is nowhere to be seen in the south of France. It's one of my go-to dishes in the summer, both because there's very little to do other than washing, cutting and mixing, so it's quick, and also because there's something about this combination of ingredients which is special. It's good food for the mind, body and soul.

———— • ————

Because of the simplicity of this dish, try to get hold of the best available ingredients; you are only cutting and assembling, so you'll get out whatever you put in. Tomatoes make up around half of the salad, so it's important that they are at room temperature: cold tomatoes taste of nothing! Cut and season them about fifteen minutes ahead of tossing the salad; they will start to gently macerate and give out a tomatoey liquid which takes the dressing to the next level.

EASY

~

Prep time 20 minutes, plus macerating

Cooking time 8 minutes

Serves 4 as a starter or light meal

~

4 eggs

Bunch of spring onions, sliced lengthways into 4–6

600g (1lb 5oz) good-quality tomatoes, at room temperature (see tip, above)

1 cucumber, deseeded

Bunch of French breakfast radishes

½ fennel bulb, finely sliced

75ml (5 tbsp) extra virgin olive oil, plus more to serve

20 Niçoise olives

300g (2 × 5-oz) good-quality cans of tuna in olive oil, drained

8 good-quality anchovy fillets

Leaves from 4 basil sprigs

Sea salt flakes and fresh-cracked black pepper

1. Start by boiling your eggs for 8 minutes (see page 82). Peel, halve and set aside.

2. At the same time, put the sliced spring onions into a bowl of iced water: they will curl up attractively. Leave them to it.

3. Cut all the vegetables except the fennel and spring onions into relatively even-sized chunks; don't worry about perfect dice or regular shapes, the more random the better!

4. Drain the spring onions. Place the tomatoes, cucumber, radishes, fennel and spring onions on a serving platter or bowl and dress with the olive oil, salt and pepper. Leave to macerate for 10–15 minutes, then give the vegetables another gentle mix.

5. There is no right or wrong way to finish a niçoise, but if you want to nerd out about it, here's the order in which I do things: sprinkle with olives, place the tuna in the centre, then the egg halves around. Drape the anchovies over the eggs, sprinkle everything with basil leaves to make it look pretty and drizzle with more olive oil and add cracked black pepper to finish.

Salmon rillettes

There's something about spreading *rillettes* over a hot grilled baguette that is so satisfying: watching it soften and melt into the toast, two become one. There's a restaurant in west London called Elystan Street which serves smoked fish *rillettes* with homemade English muffins and there aren't many weekends I don't think about going. Classically, *rillettes* are made with pork, though they can be made with many meats, poultry or fish. In all cases, the protein is slowly cooked in fat until falling apart, then shredded, seasoned and chilled. It has a luxurious, silky texture and, once made, will sit happily in the fridge for five days.

———— • ————

The smoked salmon here adds a wonderful richness. Make sure, when cooking the salmon and shallots, that the oil does not get too hot: 80°C (176°F) is plenty. Cook them in the same pan to save space, just remove the fish when cooked, as shallots will take longer to soften. An excellent starter or light lunch, this is great with crunchy radishes if you don't fancy bread, but my favourite use is as a make-ahead Christmas canapé, slathered on a blini. Beats classic smoked salmon blinis every day of the week.

ELEVATED

~

Prep time 20 minutes
Cooking time 40 minutes
Serves 4 as a starter

~

50g (⅓ cup) shallots (about 2), finely chopped

125g (5oz) salmon fillets

Olive oil (ideally), or any other oil, enough to cover the fish

125g (5oz) smoked salmon, chopped

35g (2 tbsp plus 1 tsp) mayonnaise (for homemade, see page 253)

100g (7 tbsp) crème fraîche

Finely grated zest of 1 lemon, plus 15ml (1 tbsp) lemon juice

5g (2 tsp) chopped dill

5g (2 tsp) chopped tarragon leaves

3g (1 tsp) chopped chervil, or chopped parsley leaves

3g (1 tsp) chopped chives

30g (1-inch length) of cucumber, peeled, deseeded and finely chopped

Sea salt flakes and fresh-cracked black pepper

1. Put the shallots in a small saucepan with the raw salmon on top. Cover with oil (olive oil is preferable, but any oil will work) and place over a low heat. If you have a probe thermometer (and I recommend that you do), a temperature of around 80°C (176°F) is ideal, but if not, the oil should be at the stage just before gently bubbling. Cook for 6–8 minutes, then check the salmon: you want to be able to flake the just-cooked fish. If you have a probe thermometer, its internal temperature should have reached 56°C (133°F).

2. Remove the salmon with a slotted spoon when it's ready and put the shallots back on to cook in the oil at the same temperature until very soft. Another 15–20 minutes should do the trick. Once cooked, pour into a sieve over a bowl to remove the oil, then chill.

3. The rest of the recipe is very simple from here on in! Place the cooled, cooked salmon and shallots into a mixing bowl and add all the other ingredients except the strained oil, which you can save for your next batch of salmon *rillettes*. Taste and adjust the seasoning as you like. Mix well but gently, being careful not to shred the fresh salmon too fine. Cover and chill until ready to serve.

Shellfish cocktail

A dish that's full of nostalgia for me. Whenever I eat it, I'm transported to a happy place, sitting at the table in my Christmas shirt, stinking of the new Paco Rabanne fragrance that was a gift from Nan... and then arrives the retro sundae glass of shredded Iceberg and prawns drowning in Marie Rose, and life is good. This is a great dish that's super-easy to knock up: cooked shellfish coated in a piquant sauce on a bed of lettuce in its simplest form. It's a go-to for many, especially my mum, at nearly every dinner party!

———— • ————

This is a slightly elevated version of what you may remember from your childhood family Christmas Day starter. Buy your shellfish from the fishmongers, or, if you're lucky enough to live by the sea, direct from the boat. Picked crab meat, langoustines, crayfish, brown shrimps and prawns all work perfectly, so pick your favourites and run with those. If you want to keep it simple, using only peeled Atlantic prawns will also do the trick. Marie Rose is a versatile sauce that doubles up as a salad dressing or dip, so it's never a bad idea to make a bit extra and keep it in the fridge.

EASY

~

Prep time 15 minutes

Serves 4 as a starter

~

For the sauce

120g (scant ½ cup) mayonnaise (for homemade, see page 253)

50g (3 tbsp plus 1 tsp) tomato ketchup

15g (1 tbsp) Dijon mustard

Squeeze of lemon juice

2 shakes of Worcestershire sauce

5ml (1 tsp) brandy

Pinch of cayenne pepper, plus more (optional) to serve

Sea salt flakes and fresh-cracked black pepper

For the cocktail

2 butterhead lettuces

2 avocados

Olive oil

400g (14oz) cooked shellfish (prawns, brown shrimps, crayfish, langoustines, crab, lobster, whatever you fancy!)

Chopped chives (optional)

1. To make the sauce, put all the ingredients in a bowl and mix well, then season with both fresh-cracked black pepper and a pinch of cayenne pepper. Taste: it should have a little hit of spice.

2. Carefully separate the lettuce leaves, then wash and dry them, trying to keep the leaves intact. Stack the leaves in 4 piles – larger on the bottom to smaller on the top in each case – creating 4 lettuce 'bowls'. Place these on 4 serving plates, or in glass sundae dishes. Peel the avocados and slice them, then dress with olive oil and season well. Tuck the avocado slices into any gaps between the lettuce leaves.

3. Depending on your shellfish choice, you may need to cut it into more manageable pieces. Mix the shellfish and sauce and place in the centre of the lettuce bowls.

4. To finish, I like to sprinkle mine with chopped chives, cayenne pepper, black pepper and a drizzle of olive oil. There's something very appetising about the speckles of green, red, black and gold against the baby-pink dressing.

Pâté en croûte

ELEVATED

~

Prep time 30 minutes, plus cooling and chilling

Cooking time 70 minutes

Serves 12 as a starter / Makes 1 terrine

~

* You will need a 23 x 9 x 7.5cm (9 x 3½ x 3 inches) terrine mould, or an oven dish of similar volume (1.6 litres/7 cups).

For the hot water crust pastry

550g (4⅓ cups plus 1 tbsp) plain flour, plus more to dust

220ml (¾ cup plus 3 tbsp) water

1½ tsp sea salt flakes

200g (1 cup) lard

1 egg, lightly beaten

For the filling

800g (1¾lbs) pork shoulder, coarsely minced

325g (12oz) smoked cured belly bacon, such as pancetta, diced

200g (7oz) pork loin, diced

30g (2 tbsp) garlic cloves (6 fat), finely chopped

Leaves from ½ bunch of sage, finely chopped

1 egg

Sea salt flakes and freshly ground white pepper

For the jelly

14 gelatine leaves (platinum grade)

700ml (2¾ cups plus 3 tbsp) Brown Chicken Stock (see page 266), or good-quality shop-bought stock

A dish I was too scared to attempt until I started writing the menus for Maison François. Since opening, we've made more than 1,000 of these; it's one of our signature dishes and I'm not sure what I was so frightened about! This is a French charcuterie, a delicious meat pâté wrapped in pastry and baked until golden brown (*en croûte* simply means 'in a crust'). It has been around since the Middle Ages, and, originally, the crust was only to preserve the meat inside and was not supposed to be consumed. It is now! This is best eaten at room temperature and I like mine served simply with a pile of cornichons and a pot of Dijon mustard on the side. It's all prepared and cooked in advance, making it an excellent starter, but it's equally delicious as a special lunch with a crunchy salad on the side: try it with Chicory Salad, Capers, Parsley (see page 196).

———— • ————

Planning and preparation are your friends with pâté; it's best to get organised and do everything in stages. You can make all the elements a day or two in advance, as they will sit happily in the fridge until you're ready to roll and build. The filling can include finely or coarsely ground meat, poultry or game, plus various herbs and spices. After baking, the pâté en croûte *is filled with liquid aspic, a savoury meat stock that contains gelatine, so it sets as it cools. This fills any gaps inside and keeps all the meat filling in place, but also adds a luxurious mouthfeel when eating.*

1. To make the pastry, put your flour in a mixer fitted with the paddle attachment. Bring the measured water, salt and lard to the boil in a saucepan, then pour into the flour and mix for 2 minutes on a low speed. Slowly add the egg, continuing to mix on a low speed until cool enough to handle. Tip out on to a work surface and knead for 5 minutes.

2. Take one-third of the dough and set it aside for the lid. Roll out the remaining two-thirds of dough on a work surface dusted with flour into a sheet around 5mm (¼ inch) thick. To line a rectangular terrine mould, you'll need both a main sheet 30 × 25cm (12 × 10 inches) and 2 end sheets each 12 × 10cm (5 × 4 inches). For a normal pie dish, you'll only need a base and a lid. Leave to cool. Separately roll out the dough for the lid to the same thickness, but this time 30 × 10cm (12 × 4 inches) in size for a terrine, or to slightly larger than the size of the top of your dish.

3. Place the pork shoulder in a bowl with the bacon, pork loin, garlic and sage and mix thoroughly. Season with salt and white pepper.

4. Line the terrine mould (or pie dish) with the bigger sheet of pastry, so it overhangs by 2.5cm (1 inch). Add the end pieces, if using a terrine, squeezing the overlapping seams to join securely. Now fill with the pork mixture. Top the terrine with the pastry lid and seal by squeezing the lid and base pastry together. Now the terrine is sealed, crimp the join by pinching and rolling your way around, using your thumb and forefinger.

5. Preheat the oven to 200°C fan (425°F).

6. Make 3 holes, one at either end and one in the centre, each about 1cm (½ inch) in diameter. Add a ring of offcut pastry to line each, if you like. Beat the egg with a pinch of salt and brush the pie with this mixture.

7. Bake for 20 minutes, then reduce the oven temperature to 180°C fan (400°F) and continue cooking until the internal temperature reaches 65°C (149°F) on a probe thermometer; this will take around 40 minutes. Leave to cool, then place in the fridge to chill completely.

8. Once the pie has chilled, make the jelly. Soak the gelatine leaves in a small bowl of cold water for 5 minutes and heat the stock in a saucepan until just below simmering. Remove the gelatine leaves from the water and squeeze to drain, then stir them into the stock until dissolved. Transfer to a jug, then carefully pour into the pie through the 3 holes you made (if you have a small funnel, all the better), continuing until it reaches the top of the pie. Return the pie to the fridge for at least a couple of hours for the jelly to set. When ready to serve, slice with a serrated knife and enjoy at room temperature with cornichons and mustard.

Beef tartare

Many of us who enjoy beef tartare, generally with a mountain of crisp chips on the side, know it as a restaurant dish rather than something we make at home. But it is not difficult to put together, contains no cooking (winning!) only chopping and mixing, so why don't we? I like my tartare spicy, but don't worry, this recipe is very balanced, so feel free to give it an extra hit of brandy, Worcestershire sauce or Tabasco to suit your preference. It's for that reason exactly that many good restaurants will mix your tartare tableside. Yes, there is a theatrical element too, but the truth is that us aficionados are very specific about our tartares! It's like mixing a martini: everyone has their own kinks and quirks.

———— • ————

Which cut of beef to use? It needs to be lean, so the best option is fillet. I use tail of fillet, cheaper than centre cut or chateaubriand and just as good. Putting the beef in the freezer for fifteen minutes before dicing makes it much easier to cut evenly. Leave the beef to come to room temperature before mixing and eating. The sauce doubles as a mean burger sauce, so having extra is no bad thing...

EASY

~

Prep time 20 minutes, plus freezing and bringing to room temperature

Serves 1 as a starter

~

For the sauce (enough for about 6 portions, adjust all to taste)

50g (3 tbsp plus 1 tsp) Dijon mustard

75g (5 tbsp) tomato ketchup

15ml (1 tbsp) Worcestershire sauce

3ml (½ tsp) Tabasco sauce

30ml (2 tbsp) olive oil

3g (½ tsp) English mustard

3ml (½ tsp) brandy

10g (2 tsp) horseradish sauce

For the beef (adjust to taste)

80g (6oz) beef fillet (tenderloin)

1 tsp finely chopped shallots

1 tsp finely chopped cornichons

1 tsp finely chopped capers

1 tsp finely chopped parsley leaves

About 25g (2 tbsp) Sauce (see above)

1 small egg yolk

Sea salt flakes and fresh-cracked black pepper

1. The sauce is one of my favourite recipes to type: put all the ingredients in a bowl and mix well! Taste and adjust the seasonings until it's as you like it.

2. I've allowed for the standard beef tartare mix, but if you don't like any one of the condiments (shallots, cornichons, capers or parsley), feel free to leave it out.

3. For the beef, remove any visible sinew or excess fat; your butcher can help here, but if you are using fillet, you should be fine. Place the meat in the freezer to firm up for around 15 minutes, or until it feels like you are squeezing an aubergine: firm but with some give. Using a sharp knife, chop the beef into small (0.5–1cm/¼–½ inch) dice. Leave the diced meat to come to room temperature.

4. Add your condiments and sauce to the beef, mix well and season to your liking, then taste and decide if you want more sauce and/or condiments. Spread thinly over a large plate, or push into a ring mould on the plate, gently place the egg yolk on top and hit with some more cracked black pepper. Serve with toast for a starter, or a bowl of chips and a salad for a more complete meal.

Country terrine

ELEVATED

~

**Prep time 25 minutes, plus
12 hours marinating, plus chilling**

Cooking time 45 minutes

Serves 12 as a starter / Makes 1 terrine

~

** You will need a 23 x 9 x 7.5cm
(9 x 3½ x 3 inches) terrine mould,
or an oven dish of similar volume
(1.6 litres/7 cups).*

250g (9oz) chicken livers

750g (1lb 10oz) coarsely minced pork
(see tip, right)

250g (9oz) smoked cured belly
bacon, such as pancetta, chopped
into 2cm (¾ inch) dice

10g (2 tsp) garlic cloves (2 fat), finely
chopped

1 tsp ground cloves

1 tsp freshly ground nutmeg

125g (2½ cups) fresh breadcrumbs

100g (¾ cup shelled, unsalted)
pistachios

60ml (¼ cup) Madeira

60ml (¼ cup) Cognac

10–11 Bayonne ham slices, or Parma
ham, if you can't get Bayonne

Sea salt flakes

We served this at our wedding as a starter, so it's a very special recipe to me! There's no more delicious way to kick off a meal. *Pâté de campagne*, as the French call it, is one of the easiest terrines to make at home, so it's a great dish for that upcoming dinner party. It's best prepared a few days in advance, to give the flavours time to develop. Classically, it was made from whatever leftover meat there was to hand. This recipe is the most traditional version, made from a mixture of minced pork and chicken livers. It's delicately spiced and has a velvety taste of Cognac. It's mandatory to serve this with generous amounts of cornichons, Dijon mustard and fresh crusty bread, and perhaps a dish of Celeriac Rémoulade (see page 33).

——— • ———

I appreciate that this recipe may seem like quite the production, but spread the making of it over a couple of days and it will never feel too time-consuming. Coarsely minced pork shoulder from your local butcher will do, but if you are mincing your own meat at home, chop and place the meat in the freezer for fifteen minutes to firm up before mixing, to help stop the pork from turning into a fine paste. Make the mixture two days before you want the terrine: at least twelve hours of marination is imperative to achieve the best results. The terrine only needs to reach 58°C (136°F) rather than the 65°C (149°F) required for Pâté en Croûte *(see page 46), because you want the texture here to be slightly softer, and so it should be slightly less cooked.*

1. Prepare all your ingredients. Remove the white connective tissue from the chicken livers and discard any with a green tinge, then chop into rough 1cm (½ inch) pieces. Mix your minced pork, bacon and chicken livers in a large bowl. Now add all the other ingredients apart from the alcohol and Bayonne ham and mix well so everything is evenly distributed, seasoning to taste with salt.

2. Add the alcohol and mix again. Cover with clingfilm, so it touches the top of the meat (this will prevent too much oxidisation), then leave to marinate overnight in the fridge, for at least 12 hours.

3. Preheat the oven to 150°C fan (340°F) and put a roasting dish on the centre shelf.

4. The classic terrine mould is 23 × 9 × 7.5cm (9 × 3½ × 3 inches) and this recipe fills 1 terrine mould perfectly, however you can equally use any oven dish of the same volume (1.6 litres / 2¾ pints), to save buying another dish! Line the mould with baking paper, then with the sliced Bayonne ham, leaving it overhanging by about 5cm (2 inches) all the way around. (If using an oval oven dish, you may need another slice to cover the top.) Tip in the pâté mixture, and, with the back of a spoon, press and pack the meat down into the mould, then fold over the overhanging ham to cover.

5. Cover with a lid or foil and place the terrine or dish in the roasting dish in the oven, pouring boiling water into the roasting dish to come at least halfway up the side of your pâté dish. Bake for around 45 minutes, until the core temperature reaches 58°C (136°F) on a probe thermometer. Leave to cool at room temperature before putting in the fridge, covering the top of the terrine with baking paper and adding a light weight, such as a couple of cans of tomatoes, to lightly and evenly press it overnight.

6. Once chilled and pressed, the terrine is ready to go. You can serve it in the dish it was baked in, or remove it from the mould and scrape away any fat or meat jelly from around the sides. It's now ready to be sliced and enjoyed. The finished terrine will sit happily in the fridge for 3–5 days, if well wrapped.

EGGS

·

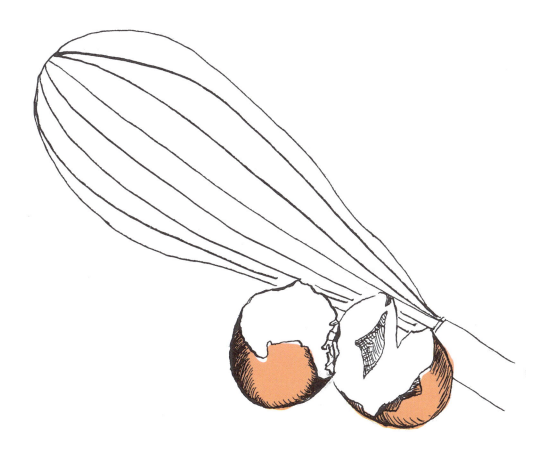

Oeufs cocotte

When I was growing up, boiled eggs and soldiers was a repeat weekend breakfast. Now I'm a little older and have to cook for myself, I've adopted this dish as my go-to instead. Not only is it more delicious, but there's also no shell to contend with! These are easy, elegant and so quick to put together, yet still feel really special. This version has onions as a base, but chop and change that to your heart's content. Serve it with toast, or baguette slices fried in foaming butter, and get ready for it to become your weekend treat, too...

———— • ————

I like to keep it simple with melting garlicky onions and soft cheese. But let your imagination run wild... bacon, mushrooms or spinach are obvious additions, but try seasonal vegetables, too. Green asparagus in spring and pumpkin in winter are both delightful. If you eat this as often as I do, it's a good idea to double or quadruple the onion base, as we do here: it's a great batch cook which holds well in the freezer.

EASY

~

Prep time 10 minutes

Cooking time 25 minutes

Serves 1

~

* You will need a heatproof ramekin for each serving.

For the onion base (enough for 4 servings)

50g (3 tbsp) butter

2 onions, finely sliced

2 garlic cloves, finely sliced

100ml (7 tbsp) white wine

Sea salt flakes and fresh-cracked black pepper

For the baked eggs

10g (2 tsp) butter

1 large spoon Onion Base (see above)

2 eggs

30g (2 tbsp) Boursin cheese

25ml (1½ tbsp) double cream

A few chives, chopped

1. Melt the butter for the onion base in a sauté pan and cook the onions and garlic over a medium-low heat until they're very soft, but without colour.

2. Add the wine and cook until completely reduced. When there is no wine left, check the seasoning and set aside.

3. Preheat the oven to 160°C fan (350°F). Place a small roasting tin inside.

4. Rub a ramekin generously with the butter, then add a portion (one-quarter) of your onion base. Crack the eggs straight into the ramekin on top of the onion.

5. Add the cheese in small chunks, then pour the cream over. Cover. (If you do not have a lid, use a piece of foil.)

6. To make sure your eggs obtain the desired wobbly-set custard texture, they need to be cooked in a bain marie. Place the covered ramekin in the roasting tin in the oven and pour boiling water into the tin to come halfway up the sides of the egg dish. Bake for 10–14 minutes.

7. When the eggs are cooked, the whites will be completely opaque. Give the yolks a gentle poke; they should be soft to the touch and the overall dish should have a satisfying wobble to it when shook. Finish with salt flakes, cracked black pepper and chopped chives. Serve with toasted sourdough soldiers if you want to keep things healthy, but I'd recommend the butter-fried baguette route every time!

Oeufs Bénédicte

You would be correct in thinking that this may not be an entirely French dish. Despite research, I'm still unclear on its provenance, but Google points me towards America. I am, however, confident in telling you that hollandaise – the undisputed star of this dish – is one of France's mother sauces (see page 274). When it's paired up with a good-quality French ham and perfectly poached eggs, that makes it enough of a French classic for me!

———— • ————

There's a lot of information out there about making the perfect poached eggs, much of it unnecessarily complex. Ignore everything you've read up to this point. It's as simple as getting two things right. First, you need the freshest eggs possible: as an egg gets older, the white becomes thinner, which causes it to break up when poaching, though a glug of vinegar helps to guard against that. The second is the temperature of the water: just before simmering is ideal, and there's no need to swirl it to create a whirlpool, just crack the eggs into the small rising bubbles.

If you are cooking this dish for a few people, I would recommend getting prepared, as we do in a restaurant setting. Make your hollandaise in advance, as it will happily sit somewhere warm for an hour. Poach your eggs ahead too, cooking them for two minutes, then putting them in iced water to stop the cooking. When you are ready to serve, toast your muffins and drop the pre-poached eggs into simmering water for ninety seconds to warm through. Top the muffins with ham, eggs and hollandaise and get ready for a world of praise from your friends.

EASY

~

Prep time 20 minutes
Cooking time 30 minutes
Serves 4

~

100ml (3½ tbsp) white wine vinegar
8 very fresh eggs (see tip, above)
4 English muffins
200g (7oz) sliced ham, ideally French ham
Butter, for the muffins
1 quantity Hollandaise Sauce (see page 259), warm
Fresh-cracked black pepper

1. Place a larger pan of water than you think you'd need for the poached eggs on to the stove to boil; the bigger the better, as that means the temperature of the water won't be affected too much when you crack the eggs into it. Add the vinegar to the pan of almost-simmering water. Once you have small bubbles coming up from the base of the pan, you're ready to start poaching. If you are cooking these ahead of time, have a bowl of iced water to hand, too.

2. Crack the eggs into separate areas of the pan and let them do their thing. They should cook for around 2½ minutes if you are eating immediately. If you are getting organised ahead of time, take them out with a slotted spoon after just 2 minutes and place in the iced water, ready to reheat when you are plating up.

3. It's pretty simple once you have all the elements ready. Toast your muffins and warm the ham (in a covered dish so it doesn't crisp up) under a hot grill. Spread the muffins generously with butter, top with slices of warmed ham and your poached eggs and spoon over the showstopping sauce. Cracked black pepper won't go amiss.

Oeufs piperade

Baked eggs are so easy to put together and delicious for a weekend brunch. This dish is based around the *piperade*, a Basque speciality made with onions, tomatoes and peppers and named after the *biber* chilli; it is one of my favourite summer recipes. *Piperade* is so versatile: if I'm not using it to bake eggs, I make it as the base for my Ratatouille (see page 193), but also like to use it as a base to braise with chicken or fish. So don't be afraid to make a bigger batch and keep it in the fridge.

— • —

To prevent the eggs from drying out in the oven, I recommend covering them with a lid. (If you don't have a lid, some loosely fitting foil will work.) This allows for gentle steaming, ensuring the yolks remain beautifully soft. You can use individual dishes and serve a portion of piperade *and two eggs in each, but I prefer making it in a large pan and baking it all together. Serve this impressive centrepiece in the middle of your table, with a crusty baguette for tearing and sharing.*

EASY

~

Prep time 10 minutes
Cooking time 30 minutes
Serves 2

~

4 eggs

For the piperade

20ml (4 tsp) olive oil, plus more to serve

90g (⅔ cups) red onion, finely sliced (about ½)

200g (2 cups) red peppers, finely sliced (about 1¼)

200g (2 cups) yellow peppers, finely sliced (about 1¼)

2 tsp smoked paprika, plus more to serve

15g (1 tbsp) garlic cloves, finely grated (3 fat)

15ml (1 tbsp) sherry vinegar

400g (14-oz) good-quality can of tomatoes

Leaves from a few basil sprigs, plus more (optional) to serve

Sea salt flakes and fresh-cracked black pepper

1. Preheat the oven to 180°C fan (400°F).

2. Place a large ovenproof frying pan – ideally one which has a lid – over a medium-high heat and add the olive oil followed by the red onion. Cook for a couple of minutes: a little bit of colour is okay, but avoid it getting too dark.

3. Add the peppers and cook for another 5 minutes. At this stage, the peppers should have released most of their water and look almost cooked. Add the smoked paprika, garlic and some salt and pepper, then cook for another 2 minutes.

4. Now add the vinegar and reduce until almost gone. Follow with the canned tomatoes and cook out for around 10 minutes. Remove from the heat and stir through the basil leaves.

5. Make 4 small indents in the mixture for your eggs. Crack the eggs into the hollows, cover with a lid or foil and place in the oven for 6–8 minutes, or until the egg whites are just set but the yolks still runny. This may take slightly longer, depending on your oven and how hot your *piperade* was when cracking in the eggs.

6. Drizzle the dish with a little olive oil and sprinkle the wobbly yolks with salt flakes, black pepper and smoked paprika. If you have some basil leaves left over and want to make things look pretty, they are a nice finishing touch.

Quiche Lorraine

ELEVATED

~

Prep time 20 minutes, plus chilling and cooling

Cooking time 55–65 minutes

Makes a 25cm (10 inch) diameter quiche

~

* You will need a 25cm (10-inch) diameter tart tin, ideally fluted.

For the pastry

450g (3⅔ cups) plain flour, plus more to dust

225g (2 sticks) butter, chopped, plus more for the tin

1 tsp fine sea salt

25ml (1 tbsp plus 2 tsp) water, plus more if needed

1 egg, plus 1 egg for brushing

For the filling

4 eggs, plus 3 egg yolks

475ml (2 cups) whipping cream

¼ tsp freshly grated nutmeg

200g (7oz) smoked cured belly bacon lardons, such as pancetta

85g (heaping ¾ cup grated) Gruyère cheese, coarsely grated

Sea salt flakes and fresh-cracked black pepper

This dish needs no introduction, but here's one anyway. It consists, of course, of smoky bacon, nutty Gruyère cheese, rich eggs and cream nestled in a buttery crust. It is one of those all-rounders that has no mealtime boundaries, fitting seamlessly into brunches, lunches or dinners. Lorraine is set in the picturesque landscapes of north-eastern France, where the dish began as a humble repast for farmers. While I offer a foolproof shortcrust pastry recipe here, store-bought pastry will do the trick for convenience seekers.

———— • ————

Whipping cream is a must if you want to achieve that luxurious set custard texture. When preparing the pastry, avoid overworking the dough, to maintain its delicate flakiness. If you don't have baking beans for blind baking, any raw rice or dried beans you have kicking around will work just as well.

1. First make the pastry. In a stand mixer fitted with the paddle attachment, mix the flour, butter and salt until they look like crumbs. Alternatively, you can do this in a mixing bowl by rubbing it all between your fingers. Add the measured water and egg, while the mixer is on a medium speed, or work them in with the blade of a knife, if making the pastry manually. Add a little more water if needed: the amount you need will depend on the absorbency of the flour, but be very careful not to add too much. As soon as the pastry has come together, turn the machine off, if using, as it's very important not to overwork shortcrust pastry. Wrap and place in the fridge to firm up for 30 minutes.

2. Preheat the oven to 200°C fan (425°F). Lightly flour your work surface and pastry, then roll out the pastry, turning the shortcrust 90° every couple of rolls. You're aiming for a nice round sheet about the thickness of a pound coin. Starting at the top of the pastry, roll the sheet around the rolling pin.

3. Liberally rub the bottom and sides of a 25cm (10 inch) tart tin, ideally fluted, with butter. Unroll the pastry from the pin over the tin and push the sides in to line the quiche. Prick with a fork all over the base, then line with baking paper and fill with baking beans (or see tip, opposite), to stop the pastry from rising. Blind bake for 15 minutes.

4. Lightly beat the remaining egg for the pastry. Remove the rice or baking beans from the pastry shell, brush all over with egg, then return to the oven for another 5 minutes or until the pastry has a nice brown colour. Take the tart case out and leave to cool.

5. Reduce the oven temperature to 130°C fan (300°F). Now make the filling. In a jug, whisk together the eggs, egg yolks, cream, seasoning and nutmeg. Once combined, stop mixing, as you don't want to aerate the quiche mix.

6. Put a frying pan over a medium-high heat, add the lardons and colour until browned and slightly crisp. Drain the excess fat and put the pancetta into the baked tart case, then cover with the cheese. Pour over most of the egg mix, leaving the last bit for when the quiche is in the oven.

7. Set the quiche safely in the oven, then top up with the remaining filling. Cook for 30–40 minutes or until the egg has just set, with a little wobble when shaken gently. It will puff slightly and turn beautifully golden on top. Leave to stand for a little while before eating; it's great at room temperature, but extra special while it's still warm.

Croque madame

This recipe takes me back to one of my first introductions to French food, while on holiday in France. My mum is trying to coax me to eat my lunch in a restaurant: 'It's just a ham and cheese toastie…!' Me: 'Why's there an egg on it?' Older and wiser now, the egg makes complete sense. If you're looking for the ultimate sandwich, this is a lesson in extravagance: white bread, butter, cheese, ham, mornay sauce (béchamel sauce upgraded with melted Gruyère) and a fried egg. It's luxurious and deeply comforting. Serve with cornichons or anything high in acidity, to help cut the richness. (Tommy K does the trick.)

———— • ————

As many delis do across France, these sandwiches can be pre-made and will sit happily in the fridge, topped with mornay sauce, ready to be grilled in a hot oven when you're ready to eat. When it comes to frying the egg, I would always suggest being generous with the butter and getting it properly hot, so your egg gets those crispy edges.

EASY

~

Prep time 10 minutes

Cooking time 15 minutes

Serves 1

~

2 slices of bread (the French would use *pain de mie*, milk loaf, but any will work)

Dijon mustard

100g (scant ½ cup) Mornay Sauce (see page 255)

80g (¾ cup grated) Gruyère cheese, coarsely grated

2 slices of good-quality ham

25g (2 tbsp) butter, plus more for the egg

1 egg

Sea salt flakes and fresh-cracked black pepper

1. Spread the inside of the bread slices generously with Dijon. Add a spoonful of mornay sauce to each slice of bread and spread it out thinly. Put half the cheese on a slice of bread, then the sliced ham, then cover with the remaining cheese and top with the other slice of bread, mornay side facing inwards.

2. Melt the butter in a small frying pan over a medium heat. Add the croque and colour slowly on both sides until crisp and golden. Meanwhile, heat the grill to high.

3. Now put the croque on to a baking tray and cover with 2 spoons more of the mornay sauce. Put under the hot grill until the sauce colours.

4. Meanwhile, in the same frying pan, melt a little more butter over a medium-high heat and crack in the egg. Cook the egg, basting it with the foaming butter to cook the egg white on top. Remove the egg from the pan and season with salt and pepper. Crown the croque with your fried egg and serve.

Galettes complètes

Though France created fine dining, and there are plenty of fancy restaurants across the country, I'd prefer a simple ham and cheese galette any day of the week. It is a thin, earthy buckwheat crêpe, topped with salted butter, smoked ham, grated Gruyère and a fried egg. The dish comes from Brittany, is completely gluten-free and makes the perfect meal.

——— • ———

When you're making the batter for these galettes, start with just over half the total amount of water and mix vigorously until you have a smooth mixture. Leave this in the fridge overnight, before adding the rest of the water just before cooking. This results in a more active batter, meaning you'll get those nice small holes all over the crêpe. Any combination of cheese, sliced meat and egg will work well here, but feel free to get elaborate, too, as you can add almost anything you fancy.

ELEVATED

~

Prep time 10 minutes, plus 12 hours chilling

Cooking time 5 minutes for each galette

Makes 4

~

For the batter

170g (1¼ cups) buckwheat flour

1 tsp sea salt flakes

1 tsp honey

340ml (1⅓ cups) water, plus more if needed

For the galettes

Salted butter, for cooking

4 eggs

200g (7oz) sliced smoked ham

200g (2 cups) Gruyère cheese, coarsely grated

10g (3 tbsp) chopped chives

Sea salt flakes and fresh-cracked black pepper

1. The night before you want the galettes, in a bowl, mix the flour, salt, honey and 250ml (9fl oz) of the measured water. Mix well, cover and leave in the fridge for 12 hours.

2. Take the batter out of the fridge 30 minutes before you start cooking. Whisk in the remaining 90ml (6 tbsp) water. You may need more, depending on the flour, as you don't want the batter to be too thick, or you won't get bubbles in your crêpes. You should be able to swirl the batter around the pan using only gravity and some shaking.

3. Heat a crêpe pan or large nonstick frying pan over a medium heat. Once hot, add a small cube of butter and leave to melt. Wipe the butter evenly around the pan with kitchen paper, so there is a good even, buttery coating. Add a ladle of one-quarter of the crêpe batter and shake to evenly cover the pan.

4. When the batter has visibly set and small bubbles have appeared (after a minute or so), crack an egg into the centre. Now pick the pan up and swirl the egg around, spreading the egg white thinly across the crêpe so it cooks rapidly, then gently re-centre the yolk and add one-quarter each of your sliced ham and grated cheese around the yolk.

5. After another minute, check the crêpe has coloured on the base. If it has, fold the rounded edges towards the centre to create a square window with the egg yolk sitting proudly in the middle. Season the yolk and sprinkle with chopped chives. Serve, while you repeat to cook all 4 galettes.

Omelette

The king of egg dishes – and arguably the simplest, containing in its most basic form only two ingredients, eggs and butter – is also the hardest to perfect. The French omelette is a fundamental for any aspiring cook and one of the first recipes I learned to make when I started my training. The aim is a smooth, silky sheet of egg, with no browning, that envelops a loose scrambled egg-textured centre which the French call *baveuse*.

If I'm pushing the boat out, I like to add chopped herbs: any soft herbs work well, so I'll leave it to your preference. I tend to stick with parsley, chives or chervil, but a combination or mixture of those is also great. As you're cooking the eggs slowly, the herbs can be added to the raw eggs when you are mixing them at the start.

———— • ————

I can't stress enough the importance of a good nonstick omelette pan, which is cheap to pick up and will up your omelette game infinitely. (The perfect pan for a three-egg omelette is 20cm/8 inches in diameter.) Melt the butter and cook the eggs over a medium-low heat as you would for scrambled egg; to achieve perfection, take your time and practise often. As with most egg recipes (except mousses and meringues), good-quality fresh eggs are the essential starting point.

EASY

~

Prep time 2 minutes
Cooking time 3 minutes
Serves 1

~

* You will (ideally) need a 20cm (8-inch) nonstick frying pan.

3 eggs
Pinch of chopped herbs, such as chervil, chives or parsley leaves (optional, see recipe introduction)
10g (2 tsp) butter, plus more to serve
Sea salt flakes and fresh-cracked black pepper

1. Crack your eggs into a small bowl. I use a flat surface for cracking my eggs, which avoids small shards of shell getting in your omelette. Using a fork, to avoid aerating your eggs, whisk them with salt and pepper, adding the chopped herbs, if using.

2. Place a 20cm (8-inch) nonstick pan over a medium heat, add your butter and shake until completely melted and foaming. Add your whisked eggs and cook slowly, using a spatula to move everything around until you have soft scrambled egg in the pan. (Take the pan off the heat if it's cooking too quickly.)

3. Once you have a scrambled egg consistency, leave the pan over a low heat: this is the stage when you are making the exterior silky sheet of egg to house the soft centre. After 10–20 seconds you should be able to roll the omelette and turn it out on to a plate, aiming for a cigar shape. Rub with a small knob of cold butter once finished, to give your omelette an irresistible shine, then serve immediately.

Twice-cooked cheese soufflés

ELEVATED

~

Prep time 15 minutes
Cooking time 35 minutes
Serves 6 as a starter or light meal

~

* You will need 6 ovenproof ramekins.

For the cheese base

30g (2 tbsp) butter

30g (2½ tbsp) plain flour

140ml (½ cup plus 1 tbsp) whole milk

Freshly grated nutmeg

140g (scant 1½ cups) Comté cheese, coarsely grated

4 large egg yolks

60ml (4 tbsp) double cream

25g (1 tbsp plus 2 tsp) Dijon mustard

Sea salt flakes and fresh-cracked black pepper

For the sauce

75g (5 tbsp) butter

1 large leek, finely sliced

1 large garlic clove, finely grated

300ml (1¼ cups) double cream

120g (4¼oz) Camembert cheese, chopped

To finish the soufflés

Softened butter, for the ramekins

300g (1¼ cups) egg whites (about 9)

Lemon juice

315g (1¼ cups plus 1 tbsp) Cheese Base (see above)

A classic that never goes out of style. Cheese soufflé is constructed of two main elements: a béchamel that has been enriched with (in this version) Comté, egg yolks and Dijon, which gives a little sharp complexity; then stiffened egg whites. The two are carefully folded together, then baked, resulting in light and airy soufflés bursting with cheesy flavour. My twice-baked soufflés make an elegant dinner party starter which is simple to prepare ahead of time, best served with a tomato salad (see page 208 for my version with a vierge dressing) and a crusty baguette.

———— • ————

Soufflés have long been surrounded by an aura of fear: fear of both difficulty and of deflation! But this recipe has yet to fail me; with a little care and attention, it's easy to pull off every time. When you're separating the egg whites and yolks, it's important that no yolks are broken, as yolks (or greasy utensils, for that matter) will stop the whites from aerating properly. The temperature of the cheese base is also key: it should be ever-so-slightly warmer than room temperature, as this makes folding the two mixes together easier, resulting in a lighter finished soufflé. It's the cheese and leek sauce draped over the finished dish that makes this the decadent crowd-pleaser that it is. If you want to double up the cheese base recipe, it holds well in the fridge and freezer; you'll just need to gently heat it before mixing your soufflés.

1. Start with the cheese base. In a saucepan over a medium heat, melt the butter, add the flour and cook for a few minutes. Once the roux is cooked out, add the milk in stages as you would for Béchamel (see page 255). Bring the finished sauce to the boil while whisking, then reduce the heat and simmer for 2 minutes.

2. Grate in some nutmeg, add the cheese, season and mix until fully combined. Put the finished sauce into a blender and, with the motor running, add your egg yolks, one at a time, blending until smooth. Add the cream and Dijon and blend briefly to combine. If you are making a double batch, weigh the finished sauce into 315g (11oz) bags, so they are ready to go for a 6-portion soufflé recipe. (You can drop a defrosted bag into hot water to warm the base up when you are ready to cook.)

3. The cheesy leek sauce can be made ahead of time too. Put the butter in a saucepan over a medium-low heat and add the leek and garlic, cooking them without colour. Once completely soft, season and add the cream and Camembert. Leave to bubble for a couple of minutes until the cheese has melted, then set aside.

4. Rub 6 ramekins generously with soft butter and preheat the oven to 150°C fan (340°F), with a roasting tin inside.

5. Using electric beaters, whisk the egg whites to stiff peaks with a few drops of lemon juice to strengthen the egg whites. When the whites are completely firm, add one-third of them to the slightly-warmer-than-room temperature cheese base and beat to lighten the mix (no need to be too careful at this stage). Add the remaining egg whites and, this time, gently fold them in, using a figure of '8' shape to your folding.

6. Spoon into the buttered ramekins and tap to flatten the tops. Place in the roasting tin in the oven, pouring boiling water into the tin to come halfway up the sides of the ramekins. Bake for 12–16 minutes; it may take up to 20 minutes in larger moulds. When the soufflés are cooked, the tops will be golden brown, the soufflés will visibly be coming away from the side of the ramekins and they should have minimal wobble.

7. Turn the cooked soufflés out of the ramekins on to a baking tray. They will sit happily at room temperature at this stage, ready to be finished when you are ready to eat.

8. When you want to eat, preheat the oven to 220°C fan (475°F). Pour the cheesy leek sauce over the soufflés and put back into the oven for around 5 minutes, until gratinated all over. Serve straight away.

Oeufs mayonnaise

Once on the brink of extinction, this dish is now enjoying a well-deserved comeback, as it's an unexpected culinary pleasure. Found in every bistro across France, it seems very plain on the surface (boiled eggs and mayo? No thanks), but it's unassumingly elegant and absolutely delicious. It somehow transcends the sum of its eggy parts, especially when eaten with a basket of crusty bread and perhaps a dish of *Carottes Râpées* (see page 32).

———— • ————

Don't give in to the temptation of shop-bought mayonnaise! Homemade mayonnaise is surprisingly easy to make and key to the elegance of this dish, especially when seasoned heavily with Dijon mustard. For perfect jammy yolks, cook your eggs straight from the fridge, with a good glug of vinegar and pinch of salt. Boil for 8 minutes, then plunge them into iced water to stop the cooking.

EASY

~

Prep time 10 minutes, plus cooling
Cooking time 10 minutes
Serves 4

~

6 eggs

20ml (4 tsp) white wine vinegar

1 quantity homemade Mayonnaise (see page 253), made with 2 tbsp Dijon mustard and the juice of ½ lemon

Pinch of chopped chives (optional)

Sea salt flakes and fresh-cracked black pepper

1. Start by boiling your eggs. Place a slightly larger pan than you think you'd need for 6 eggs on the stove, fill with water and add a generous pinch of salt and the white wine vinegar: this will help you peel your eggs.

2. Once the water is boiling, add your eggs straight from the fridge and start an 8-minute timer. Have a bowl of iced water to hand.

3. Once 8 minutes have passed, remove the eggs from the boiling water with a slotted spoon and place straight in the iced water to stop the cooking. Once cooled, peel them.

4. Make the mayonnaise (see page 253).

5. Cut the eggs in half lengthways and cover generously with mayonnaise, adding some fresh cracked pepper and chopped chives, if you want some greenery.

FISH AND SHELLFISH

Cod with pea fricassée

Tartare sauce is one of my favourite things to eat with fish. In fact, it's half the reason why I order fish and chips. I was brought up on the 20p sachet version which I still secretly love: pure nostalgia with a Friday night takeaway. This dish is a combination of French classics, yes, but deep down it's really a creation born from my love of tartare sauce: the vibrant green stew of peas should remind you of those tartare flavours. As soon as we leave the cold grip of winter and early spring, this is the first thing I think of cooking. I've used cod here, but the recipe works amazingly with salmon or any white fish. If you prefer to fry your fish, go for it, but I think steamed cod is unrivalled, as it flakes so nicely into the fricassée.

——— • ———

In France, fricassée is the term used to describe meats that have been cooked in butter and served in a sauce flavoured with a stock of the same meat. However, it can also be used to describe a 'stew' of vegetables, peas being the most famous. I have combined the classic pea fricassée with tartare sauce flavourings for this dish; it's much lighter than the traditional version and the cornichons and capers mean it works perfectly with fish.

EASY

~

Prep time 15 minutes
Cooking time 10 minutes
Serves 4

~

4 x 180–200g (6–7-oz) cod fillets

50g (3 tbsp) butter, plus more to brush the cod

1 courgette, finely chopped

4 asparagus spears, very finely sliced

200ml (3/4 cup plus 1 tbsp) white wine

300ml (1¼ cups) stock: veg, fish or chicken, you choose

320g (2⅔ cups) peas, fresh or frozen

120g (½ cup) mayonnaise (see page 253 for homemade)

60g (¼ cup) crème fraîche

Juice of 1 lemon

1 Baby Gem lettuce, shredded

10g (4 tsp) chopped dill

20g (2 tbsp) brined capers, rinsed

20g (2 tbsp) cornichons, finely chopped

Sea salt flakes and fresh-cracked black pepper

1. Begin by preparing all the elements for this dish, as, once you start cooking, it comes together quickly. Fill a steamer base with water and bring to the boil, then brush the fish with butter, season with salt and pepper, place on baking paper and put into the steamer basket. Cover and steam for 6–8 minutes. Once cooked, remove the fish from the steamer and leave to rest for a minute.

2. Meanwhile, quickly bring the sauce together. Melt the butter in a saucepan over a medium heat and sweat the courgette and asparagus for 2 minutes. Add the white wine and rapidly reduce until almost completely gone. Add the stock and bring to the boil, reduce by half, then follow with the peas and simmer for 1 minute.

3. To finish the sauce, add all the remaining ingredients, bring to the boil and check the seasoning. Plate up the pea fricassée on warmed plates or a serving platter, followed by the steamed cod.

Coquilles Saint Jacques

EASY

~

Prep time 20 minutes
Cooking time 85 minutes
Serves 3

~

* You will need a piping bag.

For the mash

2 large floury potatoes, ideally Maris Piper or Yukon Gold

50g (3 tbsp) butter

20ml (4 tsp) whole milk

1 egg yolk

Sea salt flakes

Rock salt

For the scallops

9 hand-dived scallops, with their curved shells

1 shallot, finely sliced

Knob of butter

75g (1 cup) mushrooms, finely sliced

2 garlic cloves, finely sliced

100ml (7 tbsp) Noilly Prat (white vermouth)

250ml (1 cup) fish stock (see page 262 for homemade)

100ml (7 tbsp) double cream

Finely grated zest and juice of ½ lemon

5g (2 tsp) chopped chives

5g (2 tsp) chopped parsley leaves

Olive oil

For the beurre manié (see page 272)

30g (2 tbsp) butter, softened

30g (2½ tbsp) plain flour

If I was to try and explain these to a friend who had very little cooking knowledge, I'd describe them as mini scallop fish pies, served inside their shells. Properly boujee fish pie! As far as I'm concerned, scallops are the king of the ocean when it comes to shellfish. Try to find hand-dived scallops if you can; they're expensive but far superior in flavour and texture to those that are available in most supermarkets. This dish is great all year round, but especially a big hit around Christmas in France, and is often the way people kick off their festive celebrations. Why not leave the prawn cocktail to one side and give it a go this year, impressing your family with some beautifully gratinated *coquilles*?

———— • ————

Overcooking a scallop is a crime, so my only tip for this recipe is this: don't f**k them up! Get a frying pan roaring hot, season the scallops and sear them in a tiny amount of oil. This should take no longer than 20 seconds; if it takes more, your pan wasn't hot enough. We are not cooking the scallops, just giving them some caramelisation, then the cooking takes place under the grill, though again just a few minutes is plenty to finish them off. Scallops are great even when eaten completely raw, so I would always err on the rare side rather than risk overcooking them. That natural shellfish sweetness and tender flesh is what makes them so special; too much cooking will turn them, instead, into fishy bouncy balls.

1. Preheat the oven to 180°C fan (400°F). Prick the potatoes with a sharp knife, put them in the oven in a baking tray on a pile of rock salt and bake for 1 hour. Once baked, scoop out the cooked potato flesh and put it through a sieve or ricer. (The rock salt can be used next time you are baking potatoes.) Add the butter, milk and egg yolk, mix well, season to taste with sea salt flakes and spoon into a piping bag.

2. Ask your fishmonger to prepare the scallops, if needed, though in most places they will already be prepped. You want the white scallop meat with orange roe attached, and you want their curved shells too. When you get home, scrub the shells clean, as these will be your serving dishes.

3. To make the *beurre manié*, mix the butter and flour in a bowl, then chill until needed.

4. To make the sauce, sweat the shallot in the knob of butter in a large saucepan over a medium heat. When it is soft but not coloured, add the mushrooms and garlic. After 3–5 minutes, add the Noilly Prat and deglaze the pan, then pour in the stock and cream and simmer for 5 minutes. Thicken the sauce with the *beurre manié*, adding small knobs little by little, whisking between each addition, until you are left with a thick sauce. Finish the sauce with the lemon zest and juice and the herbs.

5. Preheat the grill to very hot. Heat a little olive oil over a high heat in a very hot frying pan, while you season the scallops. Add the scallops and sear them on one side (see tip, opposite). When nicely coloured, place them in their curved shells, seared sides up, spoon over the sauce and pipe the potato on top, or around each scallop, as you prefer.

6. Gratinate the coquilles under the hot grill until the tops are golden brown and crisp. Serve on a platter, the shells sitting on a bed of rock salt, to stop them from moving around.

Bouillabaisse with rouille

ELEVATED

~

Prep time 50 minutes
Cooking time 2½ hours
Serves 6

~

For the soup

2.5kg (5½lbs) fish on the bone
(gurnard, red mullet, john dory)

200g (2 cups) fennel, sliced
(about ⅔ bulb)

300g (3 cups) onion, sliced
(about 1¼)

150g (2⅓ cups) leek, sliced (about ⅔)

150g (1½ cups) celery, sliced

50ml (3½ tbsp) olive oil

200ml (¾ cup plus 1 tbsp) Pernod

100g (7 tbsp) tomato purée (paste)

200g (7oz) tomatoes, chopped

0.5g (a pinch of) saffron threads
(most of 1 supermarket spice jar)

2 litres (8⅓ cups) water

For the soup additions

180g (6oz) potatoes, peeled and cut
into even pieces (about 1 medium),
plus 50g (⅓ medium) more potato

Fish fillets, from the fish above

250g (9oz) mussels, cleaned
(see page 111)

Butter, chilled

Lemon juice

½ baguette, sliced

2 garlic cloves

120g (1¼ cups) Emmental cheese

For the rouille

2 garlic cloves

50g (⅓ medium) potato from
the Soup Additions, above

3 egg yolks

Pinch of saffron threads (the rest
of the supermarket spice jar)

100ml (7 tbsp) olive oil

Pinch of cayenne pepper

Sea salt flakes

Bouillabaisse was the dinner of fishermen from Marseille long before it became the globally famous dish it is today. After a long day on the water, having sold most of their catch to local restaurants or markets, they would be left with the bony rockfish which were un-sellable. They cooked them down slowly with vegetables, spices and local tomatoes… and bouillabaisse was born. From what was once unwanted and very cheap, it is now common for the dish to cost around €50 (yes, really) for a portion of traditional bouillabaisse in Marseille. It is a rich soup, bursting with flavours of Provence: a vegetable base of onion, celery, leek, tomato and fennel is gently spiced with saffron. It is served with a spicy mayonnaise known as rouille, which is dolloped on top of croutons covered in cheese… yes, it just keeps getting better and better.

———•———

In the UK, the scorpion fish that is traditionally used to make this soup is incredibly hard to get hold of. I can also give you 350 reasons to use an English alternative, as my fishmonger hit me with quite the bill when I ordered it, direct from France, to make a recipe video for my social media. In the south of France, the dish is served in two courses: soup first, followed by the cooked fish. I prefer serving it like a fish stew, cooking the potatoes and fish gently in the soup and topping with the cheesy rouille croutons; it's all so delicious together, and, anyway, who's got the patience to wait for their fish to turn up?

1. Remove the fillets from the fish, or ask your fishmonger to do it and give you the bones. The bones need to be rinsed of any large blood clots and chopped slightly so they fit in a pan, otherwise you're good to go.

2. Separate enough skin-on fillets of fish for 6 guests and cut them into equal-sized pieces to help with even cooking. Put any leftover trimmings with the fish heads and bones for the soup.

3. In your biggest pot with the widest base, cook the sliced vegetables in the olive oil over a medium-high heat, stirring every minute; you want them to get some colour. After 5–10 minutes, add your prepared fish bones, heads and trimmings and roast for another 5–10 minutes. Add the Pernod (watch your eyebrows) and flambé with a long match.

4. Once the alcohol has cooked off and the flames subside, add the tomato purée (paste) and cook for a couple of minutes over a low heat. Follow with the tomatoes, saffron and measured water and gently simmer for 2 hours. You don't want to skim the soup as you would for a stock or sauce: any fat that comes to the top will be deep orange, giving the famous flavour and colour. If the water level gets too low, keep topping it up.

5. After 2 hours, carefully transfer the soup to a blender and blitz. It will not get completely smooth in the blender, but you are doing this to extract maximum flavour from your fish trimmings, heads and bones.

6. Pass the soup through a sieve into a clean pan and reduce it until you have a nice consistency. While it is reducing, you'll cook the potatoes and fish in the soup. Start with the potatoes (adding the extra amount for the rouille), until almost cooked. Scoop out the potato for the rouille.

7. Now for that rouille. In a mortar and pestle, smash your garlic, then the cooked potato, then the egg yolks and saffron. Move to a bowl and slowly whisk in the olive oil, as for a mayonnaise (see page 253), adding a little water if it gets too thick. Finish with some salt and cayenne pepper.

8. Add the fish fillets and mussels to the soup for the last few minutes. Now add a couple of knobs of cold butter and some lemon juice to really bring it to life. Quickly toast the baguette slices and rub them with the garlic cloves. Grate the cheese.

9. Top the garlicky baguette croutons with your homemade rouille and plenty of grated cheese. Drop at least 3 of these loaded croutons into warmed bowls of soup. Serve with the extra rouille, croutons and grated cheese on the side for a little DIY section... I can confidently say that 3 in each bowl won't be enough.

Hake with Provençal sauce

This feels like such a holiday dish, full of ingredients you'd find in a French local market, which are always that much better than the equivalent at home. (Why is that?) Sauce Provençal is simple and beautiful with any fish; I've suggested hake here, but sub in your favourite, as salmon, cod or sea bass would all work perfectly too. I like to bake the fish directly on top of the sauce: it saves on washing up, and also allows the fish juices to mingle with the sauce, making it that extra bit special.

This dish is great served with *Pommes Parmentier* (see page 178) or simply plain boiled rice, along with green salad or seasonal vegetables.

—— • ——

Essentially a fancy tomato sauce, anchovies are the secret ingredient here. If you have a fussy eater around the table, like I do, don't even mention the anchovies, as they'll never know! (Yes, Rachel, I've done this to you many a time…) When baking the fish, cover the dish with foil, to allow the steam to gently cook it, keeping it succulent, soft and completely tender. It's a great cooking technique, with the bonus that it makes it very hard to overcook the fish.

EASY

~

Prep time 10 minutes

Cooking time 30 minutes

Serves 2

~

2 x 220g (8-oz) hake portions, cut through the bone

For the Provençal sauce

240g (8oz) tomatoes, roughly chopped

30ml (2 tbsp) olive oil

60g (heaping ⅓ cup) shallots, finely chopped (about 2)

1 garlic clove, finely chopped

1 red chilli, deseeded and very finely sliced

10g (about 4) good-quality anchovy fillets

50ml (3 tbsp) white wine

20g (about 7) pitted black olives

20g (2 tbsp) brined capers, rinsed

5g (2 tsp) chopped parsley leaves

Sea salt flakes and fresh-cracked black pepper

1. Preheat the oven to 200°C fan (425°F). Put the chopped tomatoes on to a tray and season, then roast in the oven for 15 minutes.

2. Meanwhile, take a small saucepan (preferably ovenproof) and place over a medium heat, add the olive oil and sweat the shallots for 3 minutes. Now add the garlic, chilli and anchovies and cook for another couple of minutes: you'll see that the anchovy fillets will melt away. Then pour in the white wine and reduce by half. Finish with the olives, capers and the roasted tomatoes, then check and adjust the seasoning. Finish with the chopped parsley.

3. Reduce the oven temperature to 170°C fan (375°F). I leave my hot sauce in its ovenproof pan, but if your pan isn't ovenproof, pour it into an oven dish. Season your fish portions with salt and pepper and place on top of the hot Provençal sauce. Cover with foil or a lid and place in the oven for 15 minutes, or until the fish is opaque and cooked through.

4. Leave the fish to rest for a couple of minutes before serving. All in all a very versatile sauce, which I cook a lot!

Lobster thermidor

ELEVATED

~

Prep time 30 minutes, plus freezing
Cooking time 40 minutes
Serves 4

~

4 lobsters

120g (1¼ cups) Emmental cheese, coarsely grated, to serve

Sea salt flakes

For the fish velouté

50g (3 tbsp) butter

50g (4½ tbsp) plain flour

400ml (1⅔ cups) fish stock (see page 262 for homemade)

For the sauce

50g (3 tbsp) butter

40g (¼ cup) shallots, finely chopped (about 2)

100ml (7 tbsp) dry white wine

350g (1½ cups) Fish Velouté (see above)

50ml (3 tbsp) double cream

1 egg yolk

10g (2 tsp) English mustard

Pinch of cayenne pepper

10g (4 tsp) chopped parsley leaves

You can buy lobsters all year, but the best time to pick up a deal is during the summer, as calm waters and good weather (hopefully) mean more people are out fishing, which helps to bring the price down! For me there are only two ways to eat lobster: simply grilled with garlic butter and lemon juice, or as a thermidor, covered with cayenne-spiked fish velouté and grated cheese and gratinated until golden and bubbling. Serve this with chips and salad.

———— • ————

Always opt for native lobsters, as the cold water means the meat is firm, sweet and succulent: they really are the best in the world. The more quickly you can remove the meat from the shells after cooking, the easier the process will be. Plunge the hot lobsters into iced water to stop the cooking, but take them out as soon as they are cool enough to handle, as the white proteins between the meat and shell set and act like glue if they get too cold. Use scissors to remove the tail meat and a flat hard object, such as the base of a pan, to smash the claws open.

1. Put the lobsters into the freezer for 10 minutes to send them into a deep sleep, then take a sharp heavy knife and cut straight down through their heads to kill them instantly. Remove the claws by twisting them off.

2. Meanwhile, place a very large pan of salted water over a high heat and bring to the boil. Have a large bowl of iced water to hand. Cook the heads and tails (still connected) and the separated claws in the boiling water, allowing the claws 5 minutes and the tails and head just 3 minutes. Drain the lobsters and plunge straight into the iced water to stop them cooking. As soon as they're cool enough to handle, cut the bodies in half and scoop the head meat out into a small bowl (this will go to flavour the sauce). Pull out and discard the intestinal tract which runs along the back of the lobster tails. Carefully wipe the space where the head meat was. Remove the shells from the claws and cut the meat into small pieces. Fill the cleaned head shells with the claw meat.

3. Making a velouté is a lot like making a béchamel, but with stock instead of milk. In a saucepan over a medium heat, melt the butter and add the flour, cook for 2–3 minutes, then slowly add the stock, stirring all the time, until you have a smooth sauce. Simmer your velouté for 5 minutes, then set aside.

4. Preheat the grill to high.

5. Now make the sauce. In another pan, melt half the butter and sweat the shallots. Once soft, add your wine and reduce until the liquid has almost gone. Add the fish velouté, remaining butter and the cream. Take the sauce off the heat and add the egg yolk, mustard, cayenne and the lobster head meat from the small bowl. Mix well.

6. Strain the sauce into a clean bowl and add the parsley, then spoon it over the prepared lobsters, cover with the grated Emmental and gratinate well under the hot grill. Serve straight away.

Parmentier de poisson

For the topping

6 medium potatoes (about 180g/ 6oz each), ideally Maris Piper or Yukon Gold

75g (5 tbsp) butter

75ml (5 tbsp) whole milk

2 egg yolks

Rock salt

For the filling

100g (7 tbsp) butter

½ fennel bulb, chopped into 1cm (½ inch) dice

1 leek, chopped into 1cm (½ inch) dice

1 shallot, chopped into 1cm (½ inch) dice

100g (1¼ cups) button mushrooms, finely sliced

50g (4½ tbsp) plain flour

400ml (1⅔ cups) whole milk

150ml (⅔ cup) double cream

600g (1lb 5oz) chopped skinless fish fillets (smoked haddock, salmon, monkfish, halibut are all good, you decide!)

100g (3½oz) peeled prawns

100g (heaping ¾ cup) peas, fresh or frozen

10g (4 tsp) chopped dill

Juice of 1 lemon

Sea salt flakes and fresh-cracked black pepper

Fancy French fish pie. British fish pie was a weeknight meal I ate a lot growing up, though in our house it contained vibrant yellow smoked haddock, boiled eggs and frozen sweetcorn. I was happy to find out, during my training, that the French had created a version of my Wednesday night dinner which was completely delicious, with meaty fish, sautéed fennel, leeks and button mushrooms, chopped dill and lemon juice. I recently made this for my family and opened their eyes to the world of *Parmentier de poisson*; there's no going back for them now, the boiled eggs and frozen veg are a thing of the past. Give this recipe a go and up your fish pie game.

———— • ————

Any fish will work well in this pie; whatever is fresh, in season and at a fair price is a good place to start. If you've ever made a fish pie and your sauce has become watery as the fish cooked, it will have been down to the quality of the fish. (Frozen fish is a no-no when making fish pie.) If you don't have a star nozzle and piping bag to pipe your potato mix on top of your Parmentier, I would suggest gently spooning it on top and roughing it up with the prongs of a fork. Rough and random is best: the more grooves and gnarly edges, the more crispy potato bits you'll get when cooking the pie, and those are the best bits, which we always used to fight over when we were growing up.

1. Preheat the oven to 180°C fan (400°F). Prick the potatoes with a sharp knife and bake on a baking tray in a bed of rock salt for 1 hour, then remove them from the oven. Meanwhile, begin the filling.

2. Melt the butter in a wide-based pan, then sweat the fennel, leek and shallot until soft but without colour, around 5 minutes. Add the sliced mushrooms and cook for another 3 minutes. Stir in the flour and cook out the roux for 2–3 minutes. Now gradually add the milk and cream, stirring all the time, until you have a smooth sauce. You have just followed the steps for making a béchamel (see page 255), only with a few more ingredients. Simmer for 2 minutes, then add the fish, prawns, peas, dill and lemon juice. Return the filling to the boil, then take it off the heat, season to taste and pour into an oven dish.

3. Preheat the oven to 220°C fan (475°F).

4. When the baked potatoes are cool enough to handle, halve them, scoop out the cooked potato and put it through a sieve or ricer. Add the butter, milk and egg yolks, mix well, check and adjust the seasoning and place into a piping bag fitted with a star nozzle (or see tip, opposite). Pipe or spoon the potato on top of the fish filling.

5. Bake for 20 minutes, or until the top is golden brown and crisp. If the fish mix was still hot when the hot potatoes were piped on top, you could also just put it under a hot grill until the potatoes are nicely coloured, which should take 3–5 minutes.

Moules marinière

Mussels are an ingredient that signify holidays and sun (hopefully) to me. Whenever I'm away and see them on a menu, I can't help myself. My preferred way to eat them is the most traditional: as *moules marinière*, in which the mussels are steamed in white wine and served in a sauce made from the shellfish cooking liquid plus cream, garlic, shallots, parsley and lemon juice. Simple as that. This Normandy classic dish is usually eaten in restaurants rather than at home, which is a shame, because it's ridiculously simple and very quick to prepare, as well as being surprisingly good value for money. It's wonderful for a sharing starter, a light lunch or dinner, and excellent with a glass of white wine (if there's any left from the sauce) some crusty bread and perhaps a large portion of *frites*.

———— • ————

The secret here is the freshness of the mussels. A good-quality mussel has a glossy shell, should be closed and feel heavy, with no 'fishy' smell. Having a good relationship with a local fishmonger is important, as cooking great food always starts with the best ingredients. Mussels should still be alive when you buy them, so make sure your fishmonger is picking your order from a batch that was fresh in that morning!

EASY

~

Prep time 10 minutes

Cooking time 20 minutes

Serves 4

~

1kg (2lb 4oz) mussels

40g (3 tbsp) butter

2 shallots, finely chopped

3 garlic cloves, finely chopped or grated

1 bay leaf

250ml (generous 1 cup) white wine

250ml (generous 1 cup) double cream

Juice of ½ lemon

3 tbsp chopped parsley leaves

Sea salt flakes and fresh-cracked black pepper

1. Rinse the mussels under cold, running water. Discard any open shells that don't close when lightly squeezed. Remove the tough 'beards' that stick out of the closed shells by pulling them until they snap off. Not the most glamorous kitchen job, but it's an important one.

2. In a large pan for which you have a close-fitting lid, melt the butter and cook the shallots and garlic over a medium-low heat until they're very soft, but without colour.

3. Add the bay leaf and white wine and bring to the boil. Increase the heat to full, tip in the mussels, then place the lid on the pan. Steam the mussels for around 3 minutes, shaking the pan occasionally. All the mussels should be open and their plump meat exposed. If they aren't, place the lid back on and give it another minute. You want your mussels to only just open: that disappointing bowl of shrivelled mussels which we've all had in less-than-brilliant pubs comes from leaving them on the heat for too long.

4. Remove the mussels with a slotted spoon and place in warmed serving bowls, discarding the bay leaf. Quickly reduce the cooking liquid by one-quarter, then add the cream, lemon juice and parsley. Double-check you are happy with the seasoning, then pour the sauce over the cooked mussels and serve immediately.

Salt-baked sea bass

ELEVATED

~

Prep time 20 minutes

Cooking time 40 minutes

Serves 4

~

For the fish

1 sea bass, about 1.5kg (3¼lbs)

½ lemon, sliced

15g (small bunch) soft herbs, such as parsley, dill or chervil

1.8kg (scant 7 cups) fine salt (see tip, right)

10 egg whites

For the salad

1 fennel bulb, finely sliced

Handful (5g/¼ cup) of soft herb leaves, such as parsley, dill or chervil

Olive oil, plus more to serve

Lemon juice, plus more to serve

Sea salt flakes and fresh-cracked black pepper

An amazing way to cook fish. As the name suggests, it is a method of cooking which involves covering food completely in salt and baking it. The salt layer protects the fish and slows down the cooking process, so it doesn't overcook. It also traps all the moisture inside, meaning the fish gently steams in its own juices. The salt from the crust penetrates the fish skin, so it is perfectly seasoned throughout, though the skin itself will be inedible. Salt-baking is ideal for any food with removable skin. I love using it to cook whole beetroots or celeriac, a great way to make a celebratory vegetarian centrepiece. This recipe is handy if you are putting a big buffet spread together, as the salt crust retains heat, so people can come and flake off chunks of warm fish for at least twenty minutes. A simple lemon juice and olive oil-dressed raw fennel salad makes the perfect accompaniment.

———— • ————

It's worth mentioning now that this will involve more salt than you have ever used before in a single recipe. Don't worry: it's just to create the crust, the amount of actual salt in the finished dish will be minimal. As most of the salt will be wasted, go for a cheaper kosher salt or non-iodised table salt. When prepping the fish, remove the fins and gills as usual; however, for salt-baking you are better off leaving the scales on, as that will make removing the skin easier once it's cooked. Once the guts have been removed, the sea bass will be left with a perfect cavity for flavour, so here we stuff it with herbs and sliced citrus. Deliciousness coming from every angle!

1. Your fishmonger will happily take care of prepping your sea bass, as it's very simple! If you have a whole fish, remove all the fins with scissors, then, with a small cut along the belly, remove the guts and gills, wipe clean and that's it. Leave the scales on for this recipe. Fill the cavity with your sliced lemon and herbs.

2. Preheat the oven to 200°C fan (425°F).

3. In a large bowl, mix the salt with the egg whites to create a 'wet sand' feeling; you can add a splash of water if it's too dry. Now you'll need to find an oven dish big enough to fit the whole fish: a roasting dish, baking tray or large shallow casserole will do the trick. Start with a thin layer of salt mix on the base, around 1cm (½ inch) thick. Place the sea bass on top, and, with the remaining salt mix, completely cover the fish. Don't worry about making it look perfect, just make sure the fish is completely covered, as any holes mean the steam will escape so the sea bass will not gently cook in its own juices. Once covered, smooth the exterior slightly.

4. Place in the hot oven for 20 minutes, then turn the tray and return to the oven for another 20 minutes. Pull out of the oven. If you have a probe thermometer (and, as usual, I recommend that you do), pierce the salt shell and probe the fish in the deepest part of its flesh (this will be at the head end): 50°C (122°F) is ideal.

5. Meanwhile, mix everything for the salad, dressing the fennel with olive oil and lemon juice and seasoning it with salt and pepper.

6. Using a serrated knife, cut around the equator of the salt crust. Remove the top half and discard. Gently remove the fish skin, if it didn't peel away with the salt crust. Season the top of the fish with olive oil and lemon juice and flake off chunks of the cooked fish. When you get to the bone in the centre, lift it from the tail end: it should pull out whole, leaving the bottom fillet clean and ready to eat. Serve with the simple fennel and herb salad.

Sole meunière

EASY

~

Prep time 25 minutes

Cooking time 15 minutes

Serves 1, or 2 if you're feeling generous, or the fish is a good size to share

~

1 × 600g (1¼-lb) Dover sole (or see tip, right)

1 lemon, plus lemon wedges to serve

75g (5 tbsp) butter, chopped

30g (3 tbsp) shallot, finely chopped (about 1)

30g (3 tbsp) brined capers, rinsed and chopped

Pinch of chopped parsley leaves

50g (4½ tbsp) plain flour

Olive oil

20g (about 2 tbsp) peeled brown shrimps

Sea salt flakes and fresh-cracked black pepper

Before my post box fills up with angry hate mail from French food purists, I admit it: this is not the classic *meunière*, there have been a couple of Matt Ryle additions. I think this version is more delicious and slightly more interesting than the original, which includes only fish, butter, lemon and parsley. My version – which is actually very similar to sole *grenobloise* (see page 273) – has the addition of capers and brown shrimps. There are few things more enjoyable than a fresh piece of fish cooked on the bone, served with a simple sauce. Flat fish are always my go-to: turbot, brill, Dover or lemon sole will all work amazingly well with this sauce, and, when cooked on the bone, the flesh stays succulent and has a beautiful pearly sheen. Serve with some simply blanched vegetables; when samphire is in season, I recommend trying that, but spears of either purple-sprouting broccoli or asparagus would be great too.

———— • ————

I'd strongly advise getting your fishmonger to prep your fish, or do it in the garden on a table, or you'll be finding tiny fish scales for weeks, because they get everywhere! When cooking a Dover sole, treat it exactly as you would a piece of meat. Add your butter and baste until fully cooked; if the butter is browning too quickly, add some more and reduce the temperature. If you have a larger Dover sole, it might need two to four minutes on a baking tray in a hot oven once coloured on both sides, just to finish it off, but a smaller 600g (1lb 5oz) fish should cook the whole way through in a pan. Once it's cooked, you need to leave it to rest for at least five minutes. This will help when it comes to slipping the flesh off the bone: if the fish is cooked, that will happen very easily; if the flesh is still stuck firmly to the bone, give it a couple of minutes in a hot oven.

1. This is a quick dish to cook, so you want to make sure you have everything ready to go before starting! Start with prepping the fish (or get your fishmonger on it... much easier). First, you want to cut the skirts – the frilly bits – from the perimeter of the fish, using sturdy scissors. Next, you need to remove the dark skin from the fish (the white skin on the other side stays on for a classic presentation). To do this, free the dark skin at the tail end with a sharp knife, to make a flap. With a firm grip – and a couple of sheets of kitchen paper will help with this – pull the skin, by means of the flap you made, towards the head, peeling it away. Lastly, turn the fish over and remove the scales from the white skin by scraping a knife all over from the tail to the head end.

2. Prepare your lemon. Cut away a slice from the top and bottom and rest the fruit on one of these flat ends. Cut away the skin and pith from the lemon, following the curve of the fruit. Now, working over a bowl, cut very thin slices of lemon. The slices and any juice will fall into the bowl. Reserve 5ml (1 tsp) of the lemon juice.

3. Put your butter, shallot, capers and parsley in small individual bowls.

4. Put the flour on a large plate, season with salt and pepper and use this to dust the fish on both sides. Place a large frying pan over a medium-high heat and add a splash of oil. Put the fish into the hot pan, white skin side down, and cook for 3–4 minutes, then add the chopped butter and flip the fish. Reduce the heat to low and cook for another 4–5 minutes, basting the coloured white skin with the hot butter every minute. Be careful not to let the butter burn by letting the pan get too hot. Take the fish out and leave to rest on a platter, while you finish the sauce.

5. Now the butter is nut brown, reduce the heat and add all your other ingredients: the lemon slices and 1 tsp of lemon juice, the shallot, capers, parsley and brown shrimps. Bring the pan back to temperature and check the seasoning of the sauce, adjusting it if needed.

6. Once the fish has rested, the flesh should be easy to remove from the bone. To do this, you have 2 options. The braver can wiggle a spatula from the head end towards the tail, keeping it as close to the bone as possible. Remove the bone (lift it from the tail end: it should pull out whole) and replace the top fillet. The more fastidious (and/or scared) can cut the top fillet in half lengthways and remove each half-fillet with a wide-bladed knife or fish server, before removing the bone and replacing the top fillets as before. Cover in sauce and serve with lemon wedges.

Salmon en croûte

ELEVATED

~

Prep time 15 minutes, plus cooling, chilling and resting
Cooking time 40 minutes
Serves 4

~

¹⁄₂ quantity Béchamel (see page 255, you'll need 200g/scant 1 cup here)

50g (3 tbsp) cream cheese

1 tbsp Dijon mustard

1 tbsp chopped dill

1 tbsp chopped parsley leaves

Finely grated zest and juice of 1 lemon

300g (10¹⁄₂oz) baby spinach

30g (2 tbsp) butter

600g (1¹⁄₄lbs) skinless salmon fillet

2 × 320g sheets of shop-bought all-butter puff pastry (2 × 14-oz sheets all-butter puff pastry, thawed if frozen)

Plain flour, to dust

1 egg, lightly beaten

Sea salt flakes and fresh-cracked black pepper

This dish caused me a few sleepless nights during my training as a chef. It was the main course that we had to cook for our final exam and I wasn't lucky enough to have this simple recipe back then. For our exam version, we had to make puff pastry from scratch – no pre-rolled sheets for us – and also include a delicate scallop mousse which had to be sieved ('passed') to remove lumps. *And*, sandwiched between the mousse and salmon, were soft-boiled quail's eggs (which still *had* to be runny once baked). The whole thing was encased in spinach leaves that had been individually blanched and laid out flat to create a perfect green sheet. If I haven't scared you off and you're still reading, fear not: this recipe is an equally delicious salmon en croûte that takes a fraction of the time or stress to execute. It's great as it is, but if you're really pushing the boat out, White Asparagus, Beurre Blanc (see page 206) makes the perfect side dish.

———— • ————

The different elements of this recipe can – and indeed should – be prepared on separate days, to make the dish both less onerous and more successful. There are several secrets to success:

1. Make the spinach mix and sear the salmon the day before you want to build it, as you want every element to be as cold as possible, which will help when rolling it up.

2. Once rolled, you need to give the puff pastry time in the fridge before baking; I recommend a few hours. If your filling is fridge-temperature cold (4°C/39°F) when baking starts, you have a better chance of achieving crusty cooked puff pastry and a nicely cooked centre.

3. You want the final core temperature of the fish to be no more than 50°C (122°F). I really do recommend a probe thermometer for this recipe.

4. And finally, get a baking tray hot in the oven and slide the cold salmon pastry on to the hot tray for baking: that way, no soggy bottoms in sight.

1. The day before you want to serve the salmon, start by making the béchamel and leaving it to cool.

2. In a small bowl, mix the cooled béchamel with the cream cheese, Dijon, dill, parsley, lemon zest and juice. Cook the baby spinach quickly in a saucepan with a little of the butter and some seasoning. Put the cooked spinach into a sieve and strain off the excess liquid. Leave to cool, chop it through, then stir it into the béchamel mixture.

3. Dry the salmon fillet and season it with salt and pepper. In a very hot frying pan, sear the salmon on both sides in the remaining butter for no longer than 1 minute, then leave to cool.

4. Cover both the spinach mix and the salmon and chill overnight.

5. The next day, but several hours before serving, put the first sheet of puff pastry on a lightly floured surface. Place the cold salmon fillet in the centre of the pastry sheet. Spread the cold spinach mixture evenly over the top of the fish. Brush the exposed pastry rim around the salmon with some of the egg and place the second sheet of pastry over the top. Trim any excess pastry and seal the joins well, using the prongs of a fork. Brush the entire pastry with egg, score diamond shapes to decorate if you want to get fancy, then place in the fridge, on a tray lined with baking paper, to chill for at least a few hours.

6. Preheat the oven to 200°C fan (425°F) and leave a baking tray inside to get hot. Place the salmon en croûte, directly from the fridge and on its baking paper, on to the hot baking tray. Bake for 20–25 minutes, or until the pastry is golden brown and crispy. Let the salmon rest for 5–10 minutes before slicing and serving.

MEAT AND POULTRY

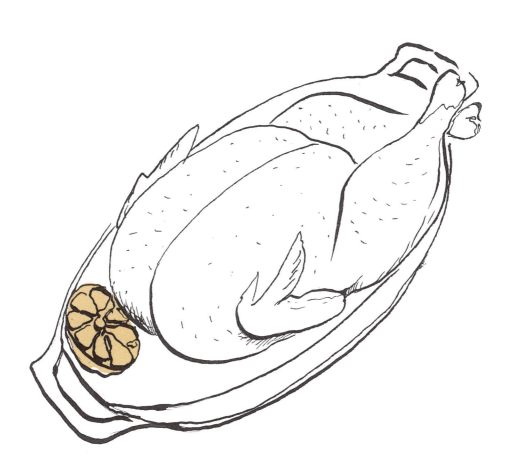

Chicken and mushroom fricassée

If you research this recipe, you'll find modern versions which sear the chicken to a golden-brown colour. However, the correct method skips this colouring. Fricassée is super-simple, even if pronouncing it is not! 'Fri-ka-say' is a rustic stew made by simmering chicken, veal or rabbit in a cream and wine sauce with mushrooms. It's comforting and easy to make on a weeknight, without any marinating or slow cooking.

———— • ————

This dish is finished with a liaison, *a mixture of cream and egg yolk that thickens and enriches the sauce. Slowly cook the chicken in generous amounts of butter and make the roux around the onions, rather than doing both stages separately; just slowly add the stock and simmer all the ingredients together. The result will be beautiful succulent chicken in a delicate pale sauce.*

EASY

~

Prep time 20 minutes
Cooking time 45 minutes
Serves 4

~

1 small chicken (1.3–1.5kg / 3–3¼lbs), or 10 chicken pieces on the bone

60g (4 tbsp) butter

½ onion, finely chopped

40g (¼ cup) plain flour

150ml (⅔ cup) white wine

600ml (2½ cups) chicken stock (for homemade, see page 263)

1 bouquet garni (see page 272)

300g (10½oz) mixed mushrooms, cleaned and sliced, quartered or halved, depending on size

2 egg yolks

100ml (7 tbsp) double cream

1 tbsp chopped parsley leaves

1 tbsp chopped chives

Juice of ¼ lemon

Freshly grated nutmeg

Sea salt flakes and fresh-cracked black pepper

1. Start by cutting your whole chicken, if using, into 10 pieces (see page 270).

2. Put a large, wide-based ovenproof pan which has a lid over a medium-low heat and add the butter. Once fully melted, add the onion and cook slowly without colour for 5–10 minutes. Add your chicken pieces, skin side down, being careful to not let the pan get too hot. After 3 minutes, flip the chicken and repeat on the other side.

3. Preheat the oven to 160°C fan (350°F).

4. Remove the chicken from the pan and add the flour to the buttery onion, then cook out for a few minutes. Now slowly pour in first the wine, then the stock, and bring to the boil.

5. Return the chicken and add the bouquet garni and mushrooms. Cover the pan and cook in the oven for around 20 minutes, or until the chicken is cooked.

6. Mix the egg yolks and cream in a small bowl. Remove the chicken from the pan and take the pan off the heat. Mix your egg yolk *liaison* into the hot sauce, off the heat, until thickened; make sure not to let the sauce boil again from now on. It doesn't need to go back over the heat in any case, as the residual heat will be all that you need. (If you were to heat it again, the sauce would become lumpy rather than lusciously thickening.)

7. Finish with the herbs, lemon juice and nutmeg, taste and adjust the seasoning, return the chicken and serve.

Dijon roast chicken

EASY

~

Prep time 15 minutes, plus resting
Cooking time 65 minutes
Serves 4

~

For the chicken

1 small chicken, about 1.5kg
(3–3¼lbs)
60g (¼ cup) Dijon mustard
80ml (5 tbsp) olive oil
Juice of 1 lemon
A few thyme sprigs
A few rosemary sprigs
1 garlic bulb

**For the garlic and herb butter
(optional)**

75g (5 tbsp) butter, softened
1 garlic clove, finely grated
Finely grated zest of ½ lemon
Leaves from 3 thyme sprigs
Sea salt flakes and fresh-cracked
black pepper

For the jus

300ml (1¼ cups) chicken stock
(for homemade, see page 263)
20ml (4 tsp) olive oil
25g (1½ tbsp) Dijon mustard
2 tbsp finely chopped parsley leaves

Roast chicken, or *poulet rôti* as the French call it, is a staple in my house, with a plate of *frites* or *Pommes Parmentier* (see page 178) piled high and a salad of crisp lettuce in simple vinaigrette. It's probably one of my favourite meals both to make and to eat. In true French fashion, mine is always full of garlic, herbs and butter.

First and foremost, success in this recipe starts with the chicken. Choose the best quality you can find: ideally, a long-limbed, slimmer, slow-grown bird. If you ever come across a *poulet de Bresse*, this is the very best. These French farmed chickens are thought to be a little tough, which I'm told is how poultry used to be! It comes from living a wonderful life running around the French countryside.

———— • ————

I start the chicken at a high oven temperature, to colour and crisp the skin, then drop the temperature, baste and cook slowly, resulting in succulent, juicy chicken with crispy golden skin. Rather than a thick gravy, I make a light sauce with the resting juices, Dijon mustard and stock, which complements the delicate flavour.

1. Make sure the chicken is at room temperature before cooking. If there's one thing I can urge you to do with meat and fish, but chicken in particular, please make sure you take it out of the fridge before you need to cook it! (Steak is the exception, see page 152.) Preheat the oven to 220°C fan (475°F).

2. Now make the butter, if using. (If you're pushed for time, feel free to skip this stage, as the chicken will be completely delicious without it.) Mix the softened butter with the garlic, lemon zest, thyme and seasoning until combined. Using your fingers, or the back of a spatula, free the chicken skin from the breast, starting from the neck cavity, to make a pocket for the herby butter. Now take the soft butter and spread it evenly under the skin. Be careful not to tear the skin, and work gently.

3. Whisk together the mustard, olive oil and lemon juice for the chicken. Rub this all over the chicken, then season with salt and pepper. Place the thyme, rosemary and half the squeezed-out lemon shell inside the cavity. Cut the garlic bulb in half and place in a roasting tray with the remaining lemon half shell, sitting the chicken on top of its garlic-and-lemon trivet.

4. Blast in the oven for 20 minutes, then reduce the oven temperature to 160°C fan (350°F) and cook for a further 40 minutes. You're aiming for the breast temperature to reach 69°C (156°F) when it's measured on a probe thermometer.

5. Leave the chicken to rest in the tray for 30 minutes, covered loosely with foil, before removing to a serving plate. Drain the excess fat from the juices, crush the garlic bulb and roasted lemon shell in the tray and add the stock. Bring to the boil and add the olive oil, Dijon and chopped parsley to make a light jus. Serve with your roast chicken.

Steak au poivre

It's rare you'll find a French brasserie that doesn't serve this dish and there's no secret about why! This is by far my favourite way to serve steak... it's always peppercorn sauce for me. I must go against the grain and suggest *Pommes Pont Neuf* (see page 172) as the perfect accompaniment to this: there's something about a chunky chip that soaks up and holds the sauce way better than a skinny frite ever can. But you go ahead and pick your favourite crispy potato accompaniment... I'll hold no grudges.

——— • ———

I read a book recently that changed my mind on how to cook steak. (It is by Tim Hayward, and, unsurprisingly, called Steak.*) It suggests two radical (for me) points: cook steaks direct from the fridge (I was told to cook from room temperature); and dry-brine overnight first (I was taught to season at the last minute). Cooking from the fridge allows the beef more valuable time in the pan for the Maillard reaction to happen, for that beefy crust to form, before it's cooked. The book suggests a last shocker: that very-volatile pepper loses flavour when heated, so, once the steak is rested, hit it with more fresh cracked pepper for maximum flavour. Give all this a go, it's really upped my steak-cooking game at home.*

EASY

~

Prep time 10 minutes, plus overnight dry-brining

Cooking time 15 minutes

Serves 2

~

2 x 200g (7- or 8-oz) sirloin steaks (strip steaks)

30g (2 tbsp) butter, chopped

1 shallot, finely chopped

1 garlic clove, finely chopped

30g (2 tbsp) green peppercorns in brine (drained weight)

100ml (7 tbsp) Cognac

200ml (scant 1 cup) Beef Sauce (see page 269), or use shop-bought demi-glace, from larger supermarkets

100ml (7 tbsp) double cream

Sea salt flakes and fresh-cracked black pepper

1. Of course you can season your steaks just before cooking, but if you have a bit of time, try seasoning them with salt 12 hours before you want to eat them. Then leave them in the fridge and, just before cooking, pat them dry with kitchen paper and add a little more salt.

2. When you're ready to cook, get a frying pan searing hot and place the steaks directly in the pan with no oil.

3. Turn the steaks every 2 minutes until they reach your desired *cuisson* (see page 271). I find medium-rare is around 5 minutes in the pan. For the last 2 minutes of cooking, you want to add the butter to the pan, baste the meat with it, then remove the steaks from the pan to rest.

4. Reduce the heat right down, and, in the beefy butter remaining in the pan, add the shallot and follow with the garlic 1 minute later. After a few minutes, once the shallot has softened, add the green peppercorns.

5. Add the Cognac (watch your eyebrows) and *flambé* (see page 273). Finish with the beef sauce and cream, reducing them to the desired consistency. Return the rested steaks to the sauce to quickly warm the outsides, then serve immediately, showered with cracked black pepper, with the mandatory bowl of chips and extra sauce on the side.

Duck à l'orange

ELEVATED

~

Prep time 20 minutes, plus freezing and resting

Cooking time 40 minutes

Serves 4

~

1 whole duck, around 1.8kg (4lbs)

25ml (1½ tbsp) olive oil

80g (½ cup) shallots, sliced (2–3)

100g (½ cup) caster sugar

60ml (¼ cup) red wine vinegar

200ml (scant 1 cup) freshly squeezed orange juice

500ml (2 cups) Brown Chicken Stock (see page 266), or good-quality shop-bought stock

1 orange, plus orange slices (optional), to serve

1 lemon

2 tbsp bitter orange marmalade

Sea salt flakes

Bunch of watercress, to serve

Ninety per cent of people will have heard of this dish, twenty per cent will have tried it, but very few will attempt to make it at home. Duck à l'orange is an absolute icon of classical French cookery, but sadly, perhaps, it's also the dish that most frequently gets bastardised. If you've eaten it in the wrong place – as I sadly did when I lost my duck à l'orange virginity – you too may have been served duck with fatty, rubbery skin drowned in an overly sweet sauce. It's enough to put anyone off. But I hope you give this recipe a go and that its deliciousness gives you renewed faith in the combo.

———— • ————

For this dish, I always roast just the crown. You could roast a whole bird, but then you have to choose between getting the legs correct or the breasts right: they won't be perfect at the same time. The trick with a duck crown is to render the fat slowly from the skin, moving the bird around the pan and pouring out excess fat as you go. If you do this stage properly, the duck won't need long in the oven; with proper cooking and resting, you'll be left with blushing rose duck breasts and thin, golden, crispy skin. It's also a lot quicker than roasting a whole bird. If you want to serve the legs too, I suggest confiting them (see page 160), then crisping them up and covering them with the same sauce, or using them for the Duck Parmentier on that same page.

1. Prepare the duck by removing the legs, wings and carcass, breaking it down into a crown (see page 270). Or get your butcher to do it all! The wings and carcass will be used for the sauce, while the legs can be saved for another occasion (see tip, opposite). Put the crown in the freezer for 10 minutes so the skin can firm up, then use a sharp knife to score the skin, to help the fat render when cooking.

2. Put the oil in a saucepan over a high heat and sear the wings and carcass until golden brown all over, then add the shallots and cook until caramelised.

3. In a separate, clean pan, mix the caster sugar and vinegar, place over a high heat and cook until you have a golden caramel, swirling the pan rather than stirring. Add the orange juice, again swirling to combine, then follow with the stock. Pour the mixture into the pan with the seared wings, carcass and shallots, then leave to slowly reduce on the stove.

4. Bring a small saucepan of water to the boil. Using a vegetable peeler, remove the zest of the orange and lemon, with minimal pith. Slice the zest into long, very thin strips and blanch them in the boiling water for 1 minute to remove the bitterness, then drain. Set aside.

5. Now remove all the pith from the orange and lemon, using a knife, and cut out the segments from between the membranes. Set aside.

6. Preheat the oven to 200°C fan (425°F).

7. Season the duck with salt and rub it into the skin, then heat a large dry frying pan over a medium-low heat. Put in the duck and brown it all over: it will colour in its own rendered fat. Take it slow: you want to render the fat as the duck colours, pouring the excess out into a bowl (save it for roast potatoes). This stage should take at least 15 minutes.

8. Place the coloured duck crown on an oven tray and roast for 8 minutes. Remove the duck from the oven, and, using a pastry brush, give it a coating of the marmalade. Put the crown back in the oven and cook for another 2–3 minutes, then remove and leave to rest for 20 minutes.

9. Place the glazed duck crown on a serving platter, putting the bunch of watercress into the cavity. Finish the reduced sauce with the blanched citrus zest and segments and pour some on to the serving platter, serving the rest on the side, adding some orange slices, if you like.

Chicken chasseur

Back in 2018, I competed in *MasterChef: The Professionals*. In the first heat, contestants have to complete a skills test. It's the first time we saw the judges, the studio and all the cameras! I was set the task of making a ravioli with sauce chasseur. At first, I froze and my mind went blank, but then managed to remember the dish and pulled off this perfect sauce. *Pommes Purée* is great with this (see page 179), or simple boiled rice.

———— • ————

Tarragon is not everyone's cup of tea, but this dish wouldn't be the same without it. A great make-in-advance meal, chasseur is perfect for a party; just follow the recipe until the chicken is cooked, then chill. Reheat it when you're ready to go, adding the tomatoes and chopped tarragon: you'll have no stress at all.

EASY

~

Prep time 20 minutes

Cooking time 70 minutes

Serves 4

~

1 small chicken (1.3–1.5kg/ 3–3¼lbs), or 10 chicken pieces on the bone

25ml (1½ tbsp) olive oil

2 onions, finely chopped

60g (4 tbsp) butter

200g (7oz) button mushrooms, halved

3 garlic cloves, finely chopped

50ml (3 tbsp) brandy

30g (2 tbsp) tomato purée (paste)

2 tbsp plain flour

125ml (½ cup) white wine

400ml (1⅔ cups) chicken stock (see page 263 for homemade)

4 tomatoes, chopped

5g (2 tsp) finely chopped tarragon leaves

Sea salt flakes and fresh-cracked black pepper

1. Start by cutting your whole chicken, if using, into 10 pieces (see page 270).

2. Place a large, wide-based ovenproof pan over a medium heat, add the oil, season your chicken pieces and colour them on both sides, starting with the skin side. Once they are coloured, remove from the pan and cook the onions for 2 minutes, then add the butter, followed by the mushrooms and garlic. Cook these for another 3 minutes, then add the brandy and cook until it has evaporated. Finally, add the tomato purée (paste) and cook for 2 minutes.

3. Preheat the oven to 180°C fan (400°F).

4. Add the flour to the pan and cook over a low heat for around 3 minutes to cook it out. Now slowly add the wine to the pan, stirring, then, once it's fully absorbed, add the stock, again gradually and in stages.

5. Double-check the seasoning and add salt and pepper if required. Return the chicken to the sauce, this time skin side up, and cook in the oven for 30–40 minutes or until the chicken is cooked.

6. If this is for a quick midweek dinner, there is no need to remove the tomato skins, but if you are being cheffy, blanch the tomatoes in boiling water for 10 seconds, then place them straight into a bowl of iced water to stop the cooking. Once cooled, peel off and discard the skins, remove the cores and seeds and chop the flesh. Add the tomatoes and tarragon to the cooked chasseur, warm through and serve.

Lamb shoulder, pommes boulangère

ELEVATED

~

Prep time 30 minutes, plus resting
Cooking time 3½ hours
Serves 4

~

* You will need a mandolin (optional).

750g (1lb 10oz) Roscoff onions, thinly sliced (or see tip, right)

50ml (3 tbsp) olive oil

3 garlic cloves, chopped

Leaves from 6 thyme sprigs

½ lamb shoulder

300ml (1¼ cups) lamb stock, or Brown Chicken Stock (see page 266), or good-quality shop-bought stock

6 large potatoes, ideally Red Rooster, or another waxy variety

40g (3 tbsp) butter

Sea salt flakes and fresh-cracked black pepper

Translating to 'baker's potatoes', this dish originates from times when people didn't have ovens in their home and bakeries might well possess the only oven in a village, a big pizza oven-style affair. This tended to take a long time to heat up, but, once hot, retained its heat. The ovens would be fired up every night to bake bread in the early morning. When the villagers went to pick up their bread, they took their *pommes boulangère* with them to bake slowly in the residual heat, ready for their Sunday lunch. These thinly sliced potatoes layered with caramelised onions, herbs and stock make a complete meal when baked with lamb shoulder on top.

———— • ————

Roscoff onions are a late-summer French speciality that I appreciate are hard to get hold of: they have an amazing rosy-pink colour, like a hybrid of a red and white onion. If you can't find them, don't worry, a regular onion will do just fine. The cooking of the onions is key to the stock, though the hunk of meat slow-roasting on top will add flavour too. You don't need to slice these potatoes too thin, as you're cooking them for long enough that the potatoes and onions should just melt into one, perfect for spooning.

1. In a frying pan, cook your onions in half the olive oil over a medium heat for around 5 minutes, before adding the garlic, seasoning and thyme. Continue to cook until the onions are soft and golden brown. If they are cooking too quickly and catching, reduce the temperature: low and slow is key here.

2. Season the lamb shoulder and sear in the remaining olive oil in a separate hot frying pan, over a medium-high heat. Once coloured all over, remove the lamb from the pan. Add the stock to the hot pan to deglaze the meaty flavour that stuck to it during the cooking process.

3. Peel the potatoes and slice thinly, either by hand or on a mandolin, anything 2–5mm (⅛–¼ inch) will work well. Season with salt and pepper and mix well in a bowl.

4. Preheat the oven to 140°C fan (325°F).

5. Get an ovenproof serving dish. Start by arranging a layer of potatoes in the base of the dish, then pour in some stock, followed by a layer of onions. Repeat the layers until all the potatoes and onions are used up. Once it's all added, the stock should come 0.5–1cm (¼–½ inch) above the potatoes. Break the butter into small pieces and distribute over the top, then lay on the coloured lamb shoulder.

6. Bake in the oven for 3 hours. By the end of cooking, the lamb should fall off the bone and the potatoes should be cooked throughout. If not, cook for another 20–30 minutes. Leave to rest for 20 minutes, then serve.

Veal cordon bleu

I'm yet to meet anyone who doesn't love schnitzel, whether of chicken, veal or beef. Let's face it, anything coated in breadcrumbs and fried until crisp is going to be delicious; it's like a giant flat chicken nugget, even the fussiest eaters can get on board with it. So trust the French to take something universally loved and improve it. I imagine the kitchen origin story went like this: 'Only one thin sheet of breaded meat? Upgrade it to two.' 'We can't just have meat and breadcrumbs, let's fill it with ham and cheese.' Boy, am I glad they had that chat. Serve with Celeriac Rémoulade (see page 33) and a pile of caperberries.

———— • ————

When joining the two pieces of meat here, use plenty of toothpicks so you have a good seal. It's also important to 'double pané' the cordon bleu (see page 274), as the egg, flour and breadcrumbs are what together create the seal that stops the cheese from leaking as it starts to melt. I prefer to shallow-fry these, as it helps with the leaking cheese situation; deep-frying causes the cordon bleu to puff up and pop like a balloon. So take your time and colour them well in a large frying pan.

ELEVATED

~

Prep time 30 minutes
Cooking time 5 minutes
Serves 2

~

* You will need toothpicks.

4 x 100g (3½oz) veal medallions, or 400g (14oz) veal loin in a single piece
8 slices of ham
4 slices of Gruyère cheese
Plain flour
2 eggs, lightly beaten
Panko crumbs
Vegetable oil
Sea salt flakes

1. If you have a single piece of loin, take a sharp knife, cut the loin in half and then both halves in half again. You're trying to achieve 4 slices with even thickness.

2. Take a slice of veal and place between 2 sheets of baking paper. Using the base of a small saucepan, or a rolling pin, gently hit the veal to flatten until you have a large circle of meat about 5mm (¼ inch) thick. Repeat to flatten all the pieces. Layer the ham and cheese in the centre of 2 pieces of the veal, leaving a 2.5cm (1 inch) border clear.

3. Place the other flattened slices of veal on top, and, using toothpicks, seal the edges with a sewing motion, going through both layers of veal the whole way around. This can be done the day before, then the meat put on a plate, covered and set in the fridge until you're ready to *pané*.

4. Place the flour, eggs and crumbs in 3 shallow dishes. *Pané* the veal in this order: flour > egg > crumbs > egg > crumbs.

5. Place a large frying pan over a medium heat and add 1–2cm (½–¾ inch) of vegetable oil. Heat until it reaches 170°C (340°F) on a probe thermometer. Cook the breaded veal in the hot oil, flipping after 2 minutes, or once the bases are golden brown. When both sides are golden brown, remove from the pan and place on kitchen paper to drain excess oil, then season with sea salt flakes and serve.

Lamb navarin

Navarin takes a cheaper cut of meat which, when cooked gently, gives meltingly tender lamb bursting with flavour. It is classically served in spring with seasonal vegetables. I remember it vividly from a traumatic lesson during my training, when a navarin I slaved over for hours burned where the old college oven got too hot. It was inedible. I had to take it to Chef, as we did at the end of every lesson, and was met with his disappointed face.

———— • ————

Chunks of lamb on the bone also work well here; I just think removing the bones makes things simpler! Take your time when colouring the lamb: if you overcrowd the pan, water is released from the meat which cools the pan, causing the meat to simmer in its juices rather than browning. Instead, colour the lamb in batches, so the Maillard reaction (see page 274) creates rich, moreish, savoury flavours.

EASY

~

Prep time 30 minutes
Cooking time 2½ hours
Serves 4

~

25ml (1½ tbsp) olive oil

1kg (2¼-lbs) boned lamb shoulder, chopped into chunks

1 carrot, chopped

2 celery sticks, chopped

1 onion, chopped

50g (3 tbsp) butter

2 tbsp plain flour

30g (2 tbsp) tomato purée (paste)

125ml (½ cup) white wine

500ml (2 cups) lamb stock, plus more if needed

1 bouquet garni (see page 272)

2 tomatoes, chopped

Sea salt flakes and fresh-cracked black pepper

To finish the stew

2 carrots, thickly sliced

8 new potatoes, halved

2 turnips, chopped into large dice

5g (2 tsp) chopped parsley leaves, or a handful of parsley sprigs

1. Preheat the oven to 160°C fan (350°F).

2. Heat the oil in a large wide-based pan which has a lid over a medium-high heat and colour the lamb pieces on all sides (see tip, above). Once you've achieved a caramelised deep brown, remove the lamb from the pan. You may have to do this in batches. Add the carrot, celery and onion and colour them. Once they are half-coloured, add the butter and allow it to foam, then reduce the heat to medium-low, add the flour and cook for a couple of minutes. Add the tomato purée (paste) and cook for 1 more minute.

3. Pour in the wine, and, once absorbed, follow with the stock in 3 stages, bringing to the boil each time. (If the sauce is too thick, you may need a splash more stock.) Simmer for 2–3 minutes, check the seasoning, add the bouquet garni and tomatoes and return the coloured lamb. Cover and cook in the oven for 1 hour.

4. Strain the sauce through a sieve into a clean pan, pick out the meat and return it to the strained sauce with the vegetables to finish the stew. Cover and return to the oven for another hour. Check the meat and vegetables are tender, then stir through the parsley and serve.

Coq au vin

EASY

~

**Prep time 20 minutes,
plus 4–12 hours marinating**

Cooking time 80 minutes

Serves 4

~

1 bottle of full-bodied red wine,
ideally Burgundy (or see tip, right)

1 small chicken (1.3–1.5kg /
3–3¼lbs), or 10 chicken pieces
on the bone

200g (7oz) smoked cured belly
bacon, such as pancetta, cut
into lardons

½ garlic bulb

1 bouquet garni (see page 272)

1 onion, chopped

3 celery sticks, chopped

1 carrot, chopped

50ml (3 tbsp) olive oil

1 heaped tbsp plain flour

200g (7oz) button mushrooms,
halved

100g (⅔ cup) baby onions, peeled

10g (¼oz) parsley leaves, chopped

Sea salt flakes and fresh-cracked
black pepper

Another great example of a dish that many will have heard of –
and many will have eaten – but few will have attempted to make
at home. Please give it a go this winter: I promise, you will not be
disappointed! This beloved recipe embodies the essence of rustic
French cuisine. It starts with bone-in, red wine-marinated chicken,
which is then braised in a luscious, glossy red wine sauce with bacon,
mushroom and onions. Similar to Beef Bourguignon in many ways
(see page 154), this dish is beautifully simple, with few ingredients
that are easy to chuck together. Time is the main ingredient that
transforms the humble elements into something truly special.

———— • ————

*The classic version of this recipe calls for red wine, specifically Burgundy,
but any full-bodied red you enjoy drinking will work well. Several regions of
France have their own version of this dish, using wines they produce –* coq
au Riesling *and* coq au Champagne *are two of the more famous – so don't
feel bad playing with different booze options! It's an ideal make-ahead recipe,
which I think tastes better the next day, or also freezes very well. Serve it with
something that will soak up that beautiful sauce: buttered egg noodles, rice,
crusty bread or* Pommes purée *(see page 179) will all hit the spot.*

1. Pour the red wine into a saucepan set over a high heat, bring to the boil and simmer for 1 minute, then leave to cool in a large bowl. This is to remove the alcohol and intensify the flavour. While the wine is cooling, move on to your chicken prep.

2. Cut your whole chicken, if using, into 10 pieces (see page 270).

3. Add the chicken to the bowl of cooled wine with the lardons, garlic, bouquet garni and vegetables. Make sure everything is fully submerged, cover and marinate for 4 hours at a minimum, or overnight if possible.

4. Pour the marinated meat and vegetables into a colander over a bowl, reserving the wine. Dry the chicken as much as you can and season with salt. Place a wide-based ovenproof pan over a high heat and fry the chicken in half the oil at a high temperature, starting with the skin side. Once browned all over, remove the chicken, add the dried lardons and cook until caramelised. Remove the lardons and finish by colouring the vegetables, then remove them, too, from the pan.

5. Preheat the oven to 150°C (340°F).

6. Add the flour to the pan and cook for a couple of minutes: it should make a roux with the rendered lardon fat and is what will thicken the sauce. Now, slowly add the red wine left over from the marination, stirring. When all the wine has been added, check the seasoning, then return the chicken, lardons, vegetables and bouquet garni.

7. Bring to the boil, cover and cook in the oven for 40–50 minutes, or until the chicken is completely cooked. Feel free to leave the vegetables in the pan at this stage, but I always remove them, so pick out the large pieces of carrot, celery and onion if you would like to do the same.

8. In a separate frying pan, cook the mushrooms in the remaining olive oil over a high heat until tender and caramelised, then follow with the baby onions and repeat. Add both to your finished coq au vin along with the chopped parsley, stir through and serve alongside your chosen carbs.

Steak Diane

How to cook a steak and to make a pan sauce for it are skills all French food-loving cooks should master, so I have included two recipes in this book, as well as steak-cooking tips (see page 271). This feels more elegant and important than *steak au poivre*... the steak you'd eat on a date. It deserves an expensive cut of beef – I always use fillet – and a more sophisticated side than chips, such as *Pommes Anna* or *Fondantes* (see pages 181 and 182).

———— • ————

I like to make big batches of Beef Sauce (see page 269) and keep it bagged in small portions in the freezer, so when it comes to steak night, it's really simple to whip up a restaurant-quality sauce with very little effort. Although homemade is always best, I concede the quality of pre-made stocks and sauces available in the shops today is the best it's ever been. A sachet of ready-made sauce can be a great option, as you'll be able to enhance the beefy-ness from cooking the steaks in the pan, while the Worcestershire sauce and Dijon mustard really help to bump up the flavours.

EASY

~

Prep time 10 minutes, plus overnight dry-brining (optional)

Cooking time 15 minutes

Serves 2

~

2 x 150g (5½oz, or 6-oz) fillet steaks

30g (2 tbsp) butter, chopped

1 shallot, finely chopped

1 garlic clove, finely chopped

80g (2¾oz) baby chestnut mushrooms, quartered

100ml (7 tbsp) Cognac

200ml (scant 1 cup) Beef Sauce (see page 269), or use shop-bought demi-glace, from larger supermarkets

1 tsp Worcestershire sauce

1 tsp Dijon mustard

100g (7 tbsp) crème fraîche

2g (1 tsp) chopped tarragon leaves

2g (1 tsp) chopped chives

Sea salt flakes

1. Of course, you can season your steaks just before cooking, but if you have a bit of time, try seasoning them with salt 12 hours before you want to eat them. Then leave them in the fridge, and, just before cooking, pat them dry with kitchen paper and add a little more salt.

2. When you're ready to cook, get a frying pan searing hot and place the steaks directly in the pan with no oil.

3. Turn the steaks every minute until they reach your desired *cuisson* (see page 271). I find medium-rare is around 5 minutes in the pan. For the last 2 minutes of cooking, you want to add the butter to the pan, baste the meat, then remove the steaks from the pan to rest.

4. Reduce the heat right down, and, in the beefy butter remaining in the pan, add the shallot and follow with the garlic 1 minute later. After a few minutes, once the shallot has softened, add the mushrooms and cook for 3 minutes or until they're cooked.

5. Add the Cognac (watch your eyebrows) and *flambé* (see page 273), then add the beef sauce and finish with the Worcestershire sauce, Dijon, crème fraîche and herbs.

6. Return the rested steaks to the sauce to quickly warm the outsides, then serve immediately.

Beef bourguignon

EASY

~

**Prep time 25 minutes, plus
4–12 hours marinating**

Cooking time 4½ hours

Serves 4–6

~

1 bottle of full-bodied red wine,
ideally Burgundy

1kg (2¼lbs) braising beef
(see tip, right)

200g (7oz) smoked cured belly
bacon, such as pancetta

2 carrots, chopped

2 celery sticks, chopped

1 onion, chopped

½ garlic bulb

1 bouquet garni (see page 272)

25ml (1½ tbsp) olive oil

2 tbsp plain flour

200ml (scant 1 cup) beef stock (for
homemade, see page 267)

Sea salt flakes and fresh-cracked
black pepper

To finish

100g (⅔ cup) baby onions, peeled

100g (3½oz) button mushrooms

10g (4 tsp) chopped parsley leaves

One of France's most famous recipes, this is a rich stew originating from Burgundy, a region renowned for its excellent wine and prized Charolais cattle. This is a dish – like so many of the classics – that started as a peasant meal made at home, a way to slow-cook tough, unwanted cuts of meat using ingredients already to hand. Over the years it has been refined. Now, it is the perfect meal if you want to impress but don't want to work too hard. All that's required is patience, to allow time and the cooking process to work their magic. Although the timings may look a little daunting, there is actually very little active effort needed during this recipe; it's only cutting, marinating, then a quick sear in the pan before the oven takes over. Plenty of time to kick back and enjoy your day.

——— • ———

Any braising cuts of beef, from chuck to short rib, would work equally well with this recipe. However, the best cut for me is beef cheeks: a little harder to find (though all good butchers will have them), cheeks give the most satisfying results, thanks to being packed with melting collagen and marbled fat. They are marinated, slowly cooked with red wine and vegetables, then finished with bacon, onions, mushrooms and chopped parsley. If you're really pushing the boat out, you can't beat proper Pommes Purée *to go alongside (see page 179). This is also a great dish to batch cook, as it freezes so well. As a quick midweek dinner, it's pretty versatile and is great with some green vegetables and a microwaved sachet of rice, if you don't fancy boiling your own.*

1. Pour the red wine into a saucepan set over a high heat, bring to the boil and simmer for 1 minute, then leave to cool in a large bowl. This is to remove the alcohol and intensify the flavour.

2. Cut the beef into pieces, aiming for 3cm (1¼ inch) cubes. Cut the bacon into lardons.

3. Put the beef in a large bowl with the lardons, vegetables, garlic and bouquet garni. Pour the cooled wine over, making sure the ingredients are fully covered. Marinate overnight in the fridge, or for at least 4 hours if you are stretched for time.

4. Pour the marinated ingredients through a sieve over a bowl and leave to drain for a few minutes, reserving the red wine. You want the ingredients to be as dry as possible, so they get maximum caramelisation in the pan.

5. Preheat the oven to 120°C fan (275°F).

6. Place a large, heavy-based pot which has a lid over a medium-high heat. Once the pan is hot, add the oil, followed by the beef, turning until all the pieces are nicely browned all over. Remove from the pot and repeat this process with the lardons, then finally the vegetables and garlic bulb, keeping the bouquet garni separate. Once the vegetables are nicely browned, reduce the temperature and evenly sprinkle over the flour, then cook for a couple of minutes, stirring constantly.

7. Gradually add the red wine to the vegetables, stirring, to form a smooth sauce that starts to thicken. Then add the beef stock in the same way. Follow with the coloured beef, lardons and bouquet garni. Check the seasoning, cover with a lid and place in the oven for 3 hours.

8. After 3 hours, everything should have begun melding together nicely. At this stage, you want to remove the vegetables from the sauce. The easiest way to do this is to place a large colander over a clean pan and pour everything into the colander. Now that the sauce is in a clean pan, pick out the beef and lardons from the colander and return them to the sauce, discarding the vegetables, garlic and bouquet garni.

9. Add the baby onions and button mushrooms to the beef, then place back in the oven for a final hour.

10. At this stage your sauce should be luscious and thick: beef completely tender and melting and all vegetables nicely cooked. Finish with the chopped parsley and serve.

Pork chop, braised butter beans

I wanted to put a recipe for cassoulet in this book, as it's so delicious. However, even as a lover of cassoulet, I've only ever made it once and I'm not sure I would again in a hurry! It's a real process, that spans more than 48 hours. So this is my cheat's cassoulet: warming, comforting and just as delicious, but which only takes 30 minutes to put together. I eat this from autumn right through to spring, as it's perfect for long dark winter nights.

———— • ————

Though I've kept things autumnal with wild mushrooms and sage, this dish works in warmer months, too. Substitute mushrooms and sage with peas, asparagus and mint in spring or tomatoes, courgettes and basil in summer. Treat yourself to a dry aged pork chop from the butcher with a generous layer of fat, at least 2.5cm (1 inch) thick to stop you overcooking the meat: pork chops don't need to be well done! Cook them to medium; a core temperature of 55°C (131°F) will give the juiciest, most delicious results.

EASY

~

Prep time 15 minutes

Cooking time 30 minutes, plus resting

Serves 2

~

2 pork chops on the bone, each 250–300g (9–10oz) and 2.5cm (1 inch) thick

50g (3 tbsp) butter

1 onion, finely chopped

3 garlic cloves, finely chopped

250ml (1 cup) white wine

250ml (1 cup) Brown Chicken Stock (see page 266), or good-quality shop-bought stock

400g (14oz) can or jar of butter beans

200g (7oz) wild mushrooms, sliced

10 sage leaves, chopped

Sea salt flakes and fresh-cracked black pepper

1. Preheat the oven to 180°C fan (400°F).

2. Start by colouring the pork chops. Place a large ovenproof frying pan over a medium-low heat. Season the chops generously with salt, then put them in the pan with the fat sides facing down, standing both side by side to give extra stability and holding them in place with tongs if needed. Here, you need to slowly cook, to make the fat melt away and the chop crisp up. Once the fat side is golden brown and the fat has rendered, increase the heat and quickly colour the chops on both sides. Remove from the pan and set aside.

3. Reduce the heat and add the butter to the pan, then the onion and garlic, gently sweating both over a medium heat. Once completely soft (about 5 minutes), add the wine and begin to reduce; after a few minutes, pour in the stock and reduce by half.

4. Strain the butter beans, reserving their liquid and adding the beans to the onions with the mushrooms and sage. Check the seasoning, place the pork chops on top and set the whole pan in the oven until your chops hit a core temperature of 55°C (131°F) when measured on a probe thermometer; this should take around 8 minutes. If the beans need a little liquid when they come out of the oven, add some of the bean stock you reserved from the can or jar.

5. Rest for 10 minutes before serving. Remove the chops, slice, then replace on top of the beans. Serve in the pan, as a centrepiece.

Duck Parmentier

I only came across this dish recently: a more interesting, delicious version of shepherd's pie. Rather than minced meat, duck legs are cooked whole, gently, in their own fat until the meat falls off the bone. A real hearty dish that I keep for cold weather.

———— • ————

To make this easy, buy your duck legs ready confited: you can find them in good supermarkets. Simply warm the legs in their fat, then flake the meat from the bones. I challenge anyone to tell the difference.

ELEVATED

~

**Prep time 20 minutes, plus
6 hours optional salting**

Cooking time 1½–3½ hours

Serves 4

~

* You will need a piping bag.

For the confit duck legs (optional)

4 duck legs

50g (3 tbsp) rock salt

5g (1 tsp) thyme leaves

3 garlic cloves, sliced

600g (2½ cups) duck fat

For the filling

4 Confit Duck Legs (see above)

50g (3 tbsp) duck fat

2 onions, finely chopped

4 garlic cloves, sliced

200ml (scant 1 cup) Brown Chicken Stock (see page 266), or good-quality shop-bought stock

3g (1 tsp) thyme leaves

10g (4 tsp) chopped parsley leaves

Sea salt flakes and fresh-cracked black pepper

For the topping

900g (2lb) Maris Piper potatoes

Rock salt

75g (3 tbsp) butter

60ml (¼ cup) whole milk

1 egg yolk

1. If making the confit, do it the day before making the Parmentier. Sprinkle a baking tray with half each of the rock salt, thyme and garlic. Put the legs on top, skin side up. Sprinkle with the remaining aromats and leave to cure for 6 hours.

2. Preheat the oven to 120°C fan (275°F). Wash the aromats off the duck and dry with kitchen paper. Melt the duck fat in a deep ovenproof pan, add the duck and place in the oven for 2½–3 hours. The meat should be easily coming away from the bones. Leave to cool slightly before removing the skin and shredding the meat. If you have gone for shop-bought confit duck legs, gently warm them in their fat so you can easily remove the skin and shred the meat.

3. Preheat the oven to 180°C fan (400°F). Prick the potatoes with a sharp knife, place them in the oven in a baking tray on a bed of rock salt and bake for 1 hour.

4. Put the 50g (3 tbsp) of duck fat for the filling in a saucepan over a medium heat and sweat the onions for 5–10 minutes until very soft, but without colour. Add the garlic and cook for another 5 minutes. Add the shredded duck, stock, herbs and seasoning. Pick an ovenproof serving dish and pour in the duck mix.

5. Increase the oven temperature to 220°C fan (475°F).

6. Scoop out the cooked potato flesh and put it through a sieve or ricer. Add the butter, milk and egg yolk, mix well, check the seasoning and place in a piping bag. Pipe the potato on top of the duck mix and bake for 20 minutes until golden brown and crisp.

Poulet basquaise

Summer in a pan. If the name didn't give it away, this originates from south-western France, born out of the Basque region's traditional agricultural lifestyle and approach to cooking. Families relied on local vegetables – beautiful big tomatoes and peppers – and often reared their own poultry. *Piment d'Espelette* is a Basque delicacy, a mild chilli dried and ground into the seasoning that makes this dish unique.

———— • ————

It's important that the sauce is cooked properly to avoid it being watery. Begin with a generous glug of olive oil and be sure not to rush any stage. The peppers need to be fully cooked before adding the tomatoes, allowing their natural sweetness to develop. Then, in turn, give the tomatoes ample time to cook off excess water before adding the chicken. You want the sauce to be thick, rich and packed with the authentic taste of the Basque region before it goes into the oven.

EASY

~

Prep time 20 minutes
Cooking time 1 hour
Serves 4

~

1 small chicken (1.3–1.5kg/ 3–3¼lbs), or 10 chicken pieces on the bone

40ml (3 tbsp) olive oil

90g (¾ cup) red onion (about ½), roughly chopped into about 3cm (1¼in) dice

1 red pepper, roughly chopped into about 3cm (1¼in) dice

1 yellow pepper, roughly chopped into about 3cm (1¼in) dice

2 tsp *piment d'Espelette* (or smoked paprika will work)

15g (2 tbsp) garlic, sliced (3 fat cloves)

1 large tomato, chopped

100ml (7 tbsp) white wine

400g (14-oz) can of good-quality tomatoes

200ml (scant 1 cup) chicken stock (for homemade, see page 263)

5g handful (¼ cup) basil leaves

Sea salt flakes and fresh-cracked black pepper

1. Start by cutting your whole chicken, if using, into 10 pieces (see page 270).

2. Preheat the oven to 180°C fan (400°F).

3. Colour the chicken pieces in a wide-based ovenproof pan with the olive oil, starting with the skin side. Once coloured on both sides, remove from the pan and add your red onion. After a few minutes, add the peppers and cook for another 5 minutes. Add salt and pepper, the *piment d'Espelette* and garlic, then cook for another 2 minutes.

4. Add the chopped tomato and white wine, then reduce until the liquid has almost completely gone. Pour in the canned tomatoes and stock, then cook them out for around 10 minutes. Remove from the heat, add the basil leaves and stir through. Return the chicken, this time skin side up.

5. Place in the oven and cook for around 30 minutes, or until the chicken is thoroughly cooked. To tell if it's ready, you can use a probe thermometer (it should have reached 74°C/165°F), or look at the chicken leg bones: when they are visible, the chicken is cooked.

POTATOES

Gratin dauphinois

If you want to make a traditional dauphinois potato, first things first: back away from the cheese! Seriously satisfying, this rich and filling dish comes from the region of Dauphiné and the authentic version contains no cheese, garlic, egg or nutmeg, despite what many recipes would have you believe. This is a crowd-pleasing side dish that pairs particularly well with beef or lamb. One of the best meals I've ever had was in an Alpine restaurant called La Soucoupe: you pick your cut of beef, the steak is cooked over a wood-fired grill, everything gets served with dauphinois potatoes to share and that's it. Incredible.

It's worth mentioning that you may need to freestyle quantities slightly here, depending on your potato size, dish size and a few other factors. This recipe has always worked pretty perfectly for me, but if you find yourself needing to add a few more potatoes, just keep the ratio of milk and cream the same (3:2 cream:milk). You want the cream mix to only just come about 5mm (¼ inch) above the top of the potatoes.

———— • ————

The potato variety is important here: Desiree or Charlotte, with their yellow waxy flesh, both work well. The next tip for mastering this incredibly simple side dish is cooking low and slow. I like to leave the potatoes in the oven for as long as possible: four hours seems to be the sweet spot. This dish will sit happily on the side for a few hours once cooked, so don't be afraid to cook it ahead of time and reheat when you're ready. Thrown together in a few minutes, the oven does all the hard work and this recipe will have people talking about your spuds for a long time to come.

EASY

~

Prep time 25 minutes
Cooking time 4 hours
Serves 4–6

~

* You will need a mandolin (optional).

1.2kg (2lb 12oz) large yellow-fleshed waxy potatoes, such as Desiree or Charlotte

300ml (1¼ cups) double cream

200ml (¾ cup plus 1 tbsp) whole milk

50g (3 tbsp) butter

Sea salt flakes and fresh-cracked black pepper

1. Preheat the oven to 140°C fan (325°F).

2. Peel the potatoes and slice thinly by hand or by using a mandolin, 2–3mm (⅛ inch) thick will be perfect. Put your sliced potatoes straight into a bowl, season well with salt and pepper and mix to evenly coat.

3. Mix the cream and milk in a jug. Begin to layer the potatoes in an ovenproof serving dish, adding your cream mix as you go: a good splash every couple of centimetres (scant inch) will do the trick. Cut the butter into small cubes and finish the top layer with butter and black pepper.

4. Cover and place in the oven for 2 hours. Remove the cover and return to the oven for another 2 hours, until nicely coloured on top and completely soft throughout.

Pommes aligot

When I have a craving for cheese, all I can think about is *aligot*. I ate this dish for the first time on a work trip to France and it's had a special place in my heart since. I'm not sure whether it should be classed as a potato dish with the addition of cheese, or a cheese fondue with the addition of potato, but this is a happy area of confusion. *Aligot* is famous for its remarkable stretchiness and it's said that a scoop of this cheesy mash should be able to stretch from the pan to the plate without breaking.

———— • ————

The secret to getting a smooth stretchy texture is in your choice of potato: use waxy potatoes and rice them, or pass them through a sieve, while they are still hot, then add cold diced butter, the cream and grated cheese slowly over a low heat. The potatoes will also need a vigorous, hard and fast beating to ensure that characteristic stringiness. The traditional recipe uses tomme fraîche, *but I've found that a combination of mozzarella and Gruyère gives a similar finished product, if you cannot get your hands on that.*

EASY

~

Prep time 20 minutes
Cooking time 30 minutes
Serves 6–8

~

1kg (2lb 4oz) waxy potatoes, such as Charlotte, scrubbed but unpeeled

115g (1 stick) chilled butter, chopped small

1 garlic clove, finely grated

240ml (1 cup) double cream

300g (10½oz) *tomme fraîche*, or 150g (1½ cups) each of mozzarella and Gruyère cheese, coarsely grated

Sea salt flakes and fresh-cracked black pepper

1. Put your skin-on potatoes into a saucepan and cover with cold, salted water. Bring to the boil and simmer for around 15 minutes or until cooked. Pour into a colander and leave to cool. When the potatoes are just cool enough to handle, scrape off the skins using a small knife.

2. Pass the potatoes through a fine sieve or potato ricer into a medium saucepan. It's worth weighing them here, so your ratios end up correct. You need 650g (1lb 7oz). Over a low heat, add the butter, garlic and cream. Using a wooden spoon or strong utensil, you want to mix the potatoes vigorously; this will help start the process of getting the potatoes stretchy!

3. Slowly add your grated cheese and keep beating until your arm gets sore. The potatoes should be smooth and stretchy enough to lift the spoon above your head without the string of *aligot* breaking. Check your seasoning and serve immediately, either straight from the pan, or transfer into warmed bowls.

Pommes pont neuf

These were the bane of my life for the first three years of my career. Who knew something as simple as a chip could cause so much pain? Turns out, when you make the best chips in town, everyone orders a portion or two, and when you put as much care into chips as I do, it seems to take over a *lot* of your time in the kitchen.

——— • ———

Chips need no introduction, but these are fancy French chips: thick-cut and triple-cooked. I like to fry mine in beef dripping, which makes them pretty unforgettable. They can be prepared in advance, up to the point just after they have been fried for the first time. You can leave them in the freezer at this stage, then they're ready to fry at the higher temperature when you want to eat them.

ELEVATED

~

Prep time 15 minutes, plus cooling and chilling

Cooking time 20 minutes

Serves 4

~

6 large floury potatoes, ideally Maris Piper or King Edward

2kg (4½lbs) beef dripping, or 2 litres (8⅓ cups) vegetable oil

Fine sea salt

Sea salt flakes

1. Peel the potatoes and cut into large chips: you're aiming for a 2cm (¾ inch) square cross-section. Place the cut chips in a bowl of iced water and wash. You can do this the day before if you like, as your cut chips will sit happily in the fridge in the water overnight.

2. Place the potatoes in a pan of fresh cold, salted water and bring to the boil. Gently simmer for around 10 minutes, or until the chips are tender and almost breaking apart. Gently remove the chips using a pair of tongs or a slotted spoon: try not to break the potatoes, but if you do, those rough half-pieces make the best chips, so keep them! Place on a wire rack, cool, then put into the fridge to dry.

3. Heat the beef dripping or oil to 130°C (266°F). Do not leave the pan unattended and on the heat; only half-fill your pan with dripping or oil and make sure your cooked and cooled chips are thoroughly dry. Add the chips for about 6 minutes, or until a fine skin has formed on the outsides. Place on a wire rack and put into the fridge to dry. At this stage, you can freeze and reserve them for another day; equally they'll sit happily in the fridge for a couple of days.

4. Heat the beef dripping or oil to 175°C (347°F), applying the same safety rules as before. This time, cook your chips until nicely golden brown all over, then drain and season with fine sea salt immediately. Plate your chips up and hit them with another pinch of salt, this time sea salt flakes.

Tartiflette

This decadent gratin of potatoes, crème fraîche, cheese, bacon, white wine and onion is true French mountain food, hard to beat as an occasional treat for a bit of luxury. Like Gratin Dauphinois (see page 168), it pairs particularly well with grilled meats, but is also a meal in its own right and can be eaten with just some beautifully dressed lettuce leaves.

———— • ————

Yes, this potato dish from the Savoie region was invented in the 1980s specifically to promote the sales of Reblochon cheese, but as that isn't the easiest cheese to stumble across, another soft cheese such as Camembert would also work well here. The name derives from the local name, tartifle, *for a type of potato (La Ratte potatoes in the UK). You can buy those in larger supermarkets, but waxy potatoes such as Charlotte or Desiree will work well too.*

EASY

~

Prep time 30 minutes
Cooking time 40 minutes
Serves 6

~

1kg (2lb 2oz) waxy potatoes, ideally La Ratte (or see tip, above), scrubbed but unpeeled

200g (7oz) pancetta

1 onion, finely sliced

100ml (7 tbsp) white wine

250g (9oz, or 8–9-oz package) Reblochon cheese (or see tip, above), chilled

300g (1¼ cups) crème fraîche

Sea salt flakes and fresh-cracked black pepper

1. Preheat the oven to 180°C fan (400°F).

2. Put the skin-on potatoes in a saucepan and cover with cold salted water. Bring to the boil and gently simmer until the potatoes are cooked. Pour into a colander and leave to cool slightly. When you're able to handle them, scrape off the skins using a small knife. Slice into 1–2cm- (½–¾ inch-) thick coins.

3. Meanwhile, cut the pancetta into lardons. Over a medium-high heat, cook the lardons in a large frying pan in their own fat until nicely caramelised. Reduce the temperature and add the sliced onion, then cook gently until the onion is soft. Add the white wine and reduce until almost completely disappeared. Check the seasoning and adjust if needed.

4. Cut your Reblochon wheel in half, to form 2 semicircles, and then cut each of these in half again through its equator (make sure the cheese is fridge-cold to help with the cutting).

5. Choose an ovenproof pan or serving dish. You want to layer your tartiflette in 2 stages. Place half the potatoes in the base, cover with half the onion mix, half the crème fraîche and two cheese semicircles. Repeat, finishing with the last two cheese semicircles on top, rind side up.

6. Place in the oven for around 20 minutes or until hot, bubbling and nicely coloured on top. Finish with some fresh cracked black pepper and serve immediately.

Pommes Parmentier

There's a chance that, without this dish, our life would not be as we know it; certainly the Earth would be a far duller, less delicious place. The French are famous for their potato recipes, but that wasn't always the case. In the 18th century, the people believed potatoes were only for animal consumption and that they could lead to a number of different illnesses. But then a Frenchman called Antoine-Augustin Parmentier was imprisoned by the Prussians, who fed their prisoner potatoes, and he realised that they were both edible and quite nutritious. When he returned to France, he created this recipe to persuade his fellow French citizens that potatoes were both safe and delicious. And, thanks to him, this book now has a chapter dedicated to the mighty spud!

———— • ————

Somewhere between a roast potato and a chip is the best way to describe these potatoes. Serve with any meat, fish, or – for the breakfast of champions – serve up with a perfectly fried egg (see page 71). The chopped herbs and garlic often struggle to stick to the potatoes, so I add a sprinkling of grated Parmesan. Not classic, no, but it both makes the potatoes taste even better and helps the herbs and garlic stick.

EASY

~

Prep time 20 minutes
Cooking time 50 minutes
Serves 4

~

75ml (5 tbsp) rapeseed oil, or good-quality vegetable oil

1.2kg (2¾lbs) floury potatoes, ideally King Edward

3 rosemary sprigs

3 thyme sprigs

3 garlic cloves

2 tbsp olive oil

20g (¼ cup) Parmesan cheese, finely grated

Sea salt flakes

1. Preheat the oven to 220°C fan (475°F). Put an oven dish containing the oil in the oven to get hot.

2. Peel and chop your potatoes into 3cm (1¼ inch) cubes. You're basically making mini cubed roast potatoes. Put them into a saucepan and cover with cold salted water. Bring the water to the boil and simmer until the potatoes are just cooked, but definitely not falling apart; this should take 8–10 minutes. Strain and leave to steam for 5 minutes, seasoning with sea salt flakes.

3. Add the cooked potatoes to the oven dish of hot oil and baste. Place in the hot oven for around 15 minutes before turning, then flip every 10 minutes until you have dark golden, very crispy potatoes. It will take about 40 minutes.

4. Pick the leaves from your rosemary and thyme, finely chop the herbs and garlic and mix with the olive oil.

5. Once the potatoes are crispy, strain off the rapeseed oil and add the herby garlic mix. Toss well. Finish with the grated Parmesan and mix gently, to help all the aromats stick to the potatoes, then serve.

For a photograph, see pages 130–131.

Pommes purée

There's a reason you can never quite get your mash at home to taste as good as the mash they serve in a French restaurant. My friends are forever asking me: how do you make the mash so great? And I'll let you into the not-so-secret secret: butter, and lots of it. In recent decades, *pommes purée* hit the news because of a top French chef called Joël Robuchon, who famously used equal parts of potato and butter! I use half the amount compared to Joël, which surely makes my mash almost a health food!

———— • ————

Yes, the secret is butter, however there are a couple more tips I need to give you to achieve luxurious, restaurant-quality mash. First, don't boil the potatoes, instead bake them whole on a bed of salt to give you the driest flesh, perfect for absorbing flavour. You'll want to buy a tamis, or a potato ricer. The classic potato masher that everyone has in their kitchen is completely useless: continually pounding potatoes will cause your mash to turn gloopy. And finally, for super-smooth mash, pass the finished purée through a sieve; the extra effort at this stage won't go unnoticed.

EASY

~

Prep time 15 minutes
Cooking time 65 minutes
Serves 6–8

~

For the dry potato mash

6 large potatoes, ideally Maris Piper or Yukon Gold

Rock salt

To finish

1kg (4 cups firmly packed) Dry Potato Mash (see above)

About 500g (4 sticks) butter

About 200ml (scant 1 cup) whole milk

Fine sea salt and freshly ground white pepper

1. Preheat the oven to 180°C fan (400°F).

2. Prick your potatoes with a small knife; this will stop them exploding in the oven. Place them on a baking tray on a bed of rock salt (any salt will work, but cheap rock salt works best and you can re-use it next time you're making mash). Bake for 60 minutes, or until the potatoes are soft.

3. Cut the potatoes in half once they are out of the oven, so steam can escape. Scoop the cooked potato flesh out of the skins and pass it through a potato ricer. Weigh the dry mash so you can get the correct amount of butter:potato (1:2).

4. Put the weighed dry potato mash in a medium saucepan over a medium-low heat. Cut half its weight of butter into small cubes and slowly add to the potato, stirring, using splashes of the milk to stop the butter from splitting. You may not need all the milk; you are just using it to bring the mash to your desired consistency and help get that butter inside. Add fine salt and ground white pepper to taste.

5. Pass the finished mash through a fine-meshed sieve, using a plastic pastry scraper, if you have one, to help push it through. This final stage is not 100 per cent necessary, but does guarantee beautifully lump-free mash.

For a photograph, see pages 156–157.

Pommes Anna

A birthday cake-shaped terrine of sliced potatoes, crisp on the outside, with a soft, buttery centre. Every time I make this, I think of sticking candles in the top of it! It wasn't until my first job at The Dorchester hotel that I actually made it (and got to enjoy the crispy offcuts when portioning it up). With just two ingredients, potatoes and butter, this recipe transforms them into something opulent, shining, elegant and seriously impressive.

———— • ————

Take your time arranging the potatoes in overlapping circular layers. I suggest using a nonstick pan, or a special pommes Anna *pan if you're going to make them often. Make sure each potato slice is evenly coated with butter and bake with a weight on top to create a compact, cohesive cake. Your slices should be pliable but not too thin, which would cause them to cook too fast. You'll need to start this a day ahead.*

ELEVATED

~

Prep time 25 minutes, plus overnight chilling

Cooking time 2 hours

Serves 4–6

~

* You will need a mandolin.

200g (¾ cup plus 1 tbsp) Clarified Butter (see page 259), melted, plus more to brush

6 medium potatoes (about 180g/6oz each), ideally Maris Piper or Yukon Gold

Sea salt flakes and fresh-cracked black pepper

1. The first baking of this dish takes place the day before you want it. Start by clarifying your butter (see page 259).

2. A nonstick tin, or oven dish with flat sides, works best, depending on what shape you want your finished Anna. I use an ovenproof saucepan and aim for a birthday cake shape. Line your tin or dish with baking paper. Preheat the oven to 160°C fan (350°F).

3. Peel and thinly slice the potatoes on a mandolin (around 1mm/1⁄24 inch thick). Put your melted clarified butter in a bowl and add the sliced potatoes as you go, seasoning with salt and pepper. As you mix, the butter might start to set, so try to leave the bowl somewhere warm, though if each slice is coated with butter, you'll be okay either way.

4. Start layering your thinly sliced potatoes in the prepared tin or dish until you reach the top. Cover with more baking paper and place a pan on top to weigh down the potatoes.

5. Bake for 1½ hours, then check: if a knife goes through the potatoes without resistance, they are ready. Cool, then place in the fridge overnight to set.

6. The next day, preheat the oven to 220°C fan (475°F). Turn the potatoes out on to a baking tray.

7. Cook for 20–30 minutes, until golden and crisp all over, brushing with melted clarified butter during cooking, for an even crisp. Serve on a sharing platter, sprinkled with sea salt flakes, then cut into wedges to share.

Pommes fondantes

Whoever created these delicious spuds must have asked themselves: what if we cooked potatoes like a piece of meat? That's the basic premise: *pommes fondantes* translates to 'melting potatoes', seared, basted with butter, then gently braised in meat stock until completely tender. If you've been to a big banqueting function, you've more than likely had a fondant potato, as not only are they easier to execute than a *Pommes Anna* or *Tartiflette* (see pages 181 and 175), but they're completely delicious and one of my favourite potatoes to elevate a weeknight dinner.

———— • ————

You'll often see these cut into perfect cylinders, but I don't like the waste! The more potato fondant the better, right? Cut the potato into oval slices, leaving their final shape for Mother Nature to decide. Always use a firm, waxy potato such as a Yukon Gold or Charlotte (or US red-skinned), which will stand up to the long slow cooking, whereas a floury potato would disintegrate. Be brave when colouring and cooking these, as darker and softer is a far better result than the opposite. And, finally, try to match the stock you use to the meat with which you plan to serve the fondants.

EASY

~

Prep time 15 minutes
Cooking time 1¼ hours
Serves 4

~

4 large firm and waxy potatoes, such as Yukon Gold or Charlotte (see tip, above)

25ml (1½ tbsp) olive oil

125g (1 stick) butter, chopped

4 garlic cloves

6 thyme sprigs, plus more thyme leaves to serve

300ml (1¼ cups) stock (for homemade, see pages 263–267), ideally to match what you are serving it with

Sea salt flakes and fresh-cracked black pepper

1. Preheat the oven to 140°C fan (325°F).

2. Cut the tops and bottoms off your potatoes lengthways, then cut into thick lengthways slices: a 3–5cm (1¼–2 inch) thick slice is perfect. Take the slices of potato, peel the outsides and soften the sharp cut edges: you're aiming for shapes that resemble oval bars of soap.

3. Place a wide ovenproof pan large enough to fit your potatoes over a high heat. Season the potatoes with salt and pepper, add the oil to the pan, and, when hot, sear both sides of the potatoes until dark brown. Some of the colour will wash off when you add the stock, so be brave.

4. Once coloured on both sides, reduce the temperature under the pan and add your butter, garlic and thyme. When the butter is foaming, baste it over your potatoes and cook for a couple of minutes. Pour in your stock; this should come two-thirds of the way up the potatoes.

5. Place in the oven to cook for around 1 hour, taking them out to baste a couple of times during the cooking process.

6. Once the potatoes are completely soft and the stock reduced, you're ready to plate up, finishing the fondants with more thyme.

Pommes rösti

When I posted this recipe on social media, a lot of angry followers told me it was Swiss and not French. Yes, this recipe comes from Switzerland, but it borders France so we are close, plus I couldn't write a chapter of my favourite potato dishes without it! If you're like me and are a sucker for the triangular hash browns they serve at a hotel breakfast buffet, this will be right up your street. I suggest topping them with a fried egg and some smoked salmon at breakfast, or a dollop of crème fraîche and some caviar at any time of day.

———— • ————

The choice of potato is important here, as a waxy potato will hold its shape much better. Cook them a day in advance if you can, as the longer you give them to chill, the longer strands you'll be able to get when grating, which helps with the form of the rösti. Take your time when cooking: the longer it takes to get to that golden stage of caramelisation, the crispier your rösti will be. And finally, be careful when flipping, as there's also a lot of hot butter involved and I've got the burns to remind me: it hurts!

ELEVATED

~

Prep time 20 minutes, plus chilling

Cooking time 40 minutes

Serves 2–4

~

500g (1lb 2oz) waxy potatoes, such as Yukon Gold or Charlotte, scrubbed but unpeeled

75g (5 tbsp) Clarified Butter (see page 259)

100g (3½oz) shallots (about 4)

Freshly grated nutmeg

Sea salt flakes and fresh-cracked black pepper

1. Put the skin-on potatoes into a saucepan and cover with cold salted water. Bring to the boil and simmer until barely cooked. Remove the potatoes from the pan, cool, then leave in the fridge to chill completely (see tip, above).

2. Clarify your butter (see page 259).

3. Slice your shallots lengthways. Put 2 tablespoons of the clarified butter in a medium pan, set over a medium-low heat and cook your shallots until soft without colour.

4. Peel the cold cooked potatoes and grate them coarsely, aiming for long strands, then put in a bowl with the cooked shallots, all but 2 tablespoons of the remaining melted clarified butter, some grated nutmeg and seasoning. Mix gently, trying not to break up the long strands of potato.

5. In a large nonstick pan, add the last 2 tablespoons of clarified butter over a medium-high heat. Add the rösti mix and form an even disc about 2.5cm (1 inch) thick. Cook slowly until dark golden brown and crisp on the bottom side. If the potato is colouring too quickly, reduce the heat. This stage should take around 10 minutes.

6. Slide the cooked rösti on to a large plate, place another plate on top and flip so the coloured side is facing up. Slide the rösti back into the pan and colour the other side in the same way. Season with sea salt flakes and serve.

Pommes sarladaises

I have social media to thank for my rediscovery of these potatoes. I was sixteen recipes into my potato classics series, and the ideas were beginning to run thin. After a quick panicked scan through my old college books, I found this dish. It sounded delicious but also very simple to make, which is always good when it comes to filming recipe videos. Potatoes are peeled, sliced and cooked all the way from raw in duck fat, then, once cooked, they're finished with garlic and chopped parsley. Simply DE-LICIOUS.

———— • ————

Very little can go wrong with this recipe, so there are only a couple of points from me. You want to make sure you are using a pan with the widest base available, so the potatoes can cook evenly in a single layer. And be patient: you want to give the potatoes ample time to make sure they are fully cooked and to soak up all that goose fat deliciousness.

EASY

~

Prep time 15 minutes

Cooking time 20 minutes

Serves 4–6

~

4 garlic cloves

Leaves from 30g (1oz) bunch of parsley (about 1 cup)

750g (1¾lbs) Pink Fir Apple potatoes, or new potatoes

150g (⅔ cup) duck fat

Sea salt flakes and fresh-cracked black pepper

1. This is a simple recipe which is quick once you get started, so start by prepping everything. Finely chop the garlic and parsley, then peel and thickly slice the potatoes: you are aiming for 1.5cm- (^{5}/8 inch-) thick potato coins.

2. Heat the duck fat in a large frying pan over a medium-low heat, add the raw potatoes, some salt and pepper and *slowly* cook and colour. Once the potatoes are nicely browned, flip and repeat on the other side.

3. Once the potatoes are coloured all over and cooked through, reduce the heat to low, then add the garlic, parsley and some more seasoning if required. Plate up!

VEGETABLES
AND SALADS

·

Leeks vinaigrette

I wasn't sure about this dish the first time I read it on a menu in Paris. It was at my first stop off the Eurostar: Terminus Nord, the big brasserie you come across as soon as you walk out of the station. Cold leeks covered in vinaigrette and eggs? Really? Leeks vinaigrette is a dish of tender leeks dressed in a tangy mustard vinaigrette, finished with herbs, croutons and chopped eggs... which, it turns out, is a match made in heaven. It is a staple of French home cooking, found on brasserie menus across the country. It reflects the French philosophy of using great produce and allowing it to shine with minimal fuss.

———— • ————

The classic preparation of leeks for this dish involves steaming, but a better way to cook them is under a grill, over charcoal, or in a hot pizza oven. By allowing the outer two or three layers of the leek to blacken completely, the inside gently steams in its own moisture, without the need for added water. This intensifies the leek's natural sweetness, resulting in a better, concentrated flavour. Additionally, the charring process eliminates the tougher outer layers, along with any grit that might have escaped washing, ensuring a tender and clean final product. There's little I hate more than a dirty leek!

EASY

~

Prep time 15 minutes

Cooking time 15 minutes

Serves 4

~

For the egg vinaigrette

1 egg

40g (scant 3 tbsp) Dijon mustard

40ml (2½ tbsp) good-quality red wine vinegar, ideally Cabernet Sauvignon

Juice of ¼ lemon

¼ garlic clove, finely grated

170ml (scant ¾ cup) rapeseed oil, or other good-quality vegetable oil

5g (2 tsp) chopped parsley leaves

Sea salt flakes and fresh-cracked black pepper

For the leeks and to serve

8 leeks

Olive oil

Croutons (see page 36)

Finely grated lemon zest

Chopped chives

1. Boil the egg in boiling, salted water for 10 minutes. Run under a cold tap to stop it cooking, then peel. Grate the yolk and finely chop the white.

2. In a bowl, mix the Dijon, vinegar, lemon juice and garlic. Now, while whisking slowly, add the oil in a very thin stream, as if you were making a mayonnaise (see page 253). Once it is thick, finish with some seasoning, the egg and parsley. Set aside while you cook the leeks.

3. Preheat the grill to hot. Peel the outer layer from the leeks and trim off any excess dark green leaves at the top. Wash thoroughly and dry. Season the leeks with oil, salt and pepper, place on a large baking tray and set under the hot grill, turning the leeks every 3–5 minutes until completely black all over. (This can also be done in a pizza oven, or over a charcoal grill.)

4. Leave the leeks to cool down slightly, then peel away the black outer layers to reveal the sweet, cooked centres.

5. Place a couple of spoons of the dressing on a large sharing platter, followed by the cooked leeks, then top with the remaining egg vinaigrette, croutons, lemon zest, chives and a little olive oil to serve.

Ratatouille, sauce pistou

I'm typing up this recipe while sitting in the sun, it's 31°C (88°F) and there isn't a cloud in the sky. I may or may not have a glass of rosé in my hand too. Both of which seem pretty fitting for this delicious recipe. Ratatouille is a Provençal dish of stewed vegetables that originated in Nice and it screams 'summer' to me. It's never out of place set proudly on a sunny table among friends, ready for sharing. It can be served in a bowl as a summery vegetable stew, but I have made a slightly fancier version here, served with *sauce pistou*, which is basically a French pesto. Both *piperade* and *pistou* can be made a couple of days in advance, leaving you to only build and bake when you decide to make the dish.

———— • ————

The secret to a special ratatouille is to use piperade *instead of plain old canned tomatoes. Piperade is made from sautéed peppers, tomatoes and paprika; mine also has basil and vinegar, which helps to give it zing. I've given another version of* pistou *on page 26, but this contains different ratios and gives a more fragrant sauce.*

EASY

~

Prep time 20 minutes
Cooking time 65 minutes
Serves 4

~

For the ratatouille
1 quantity *Piperade* (see page 65)
2 courgettes
1 aubergine
4 tomatoes
Olive oil
Sea salt flakes and fresh-cracked black pepper

For the sauce pistou (optional)
70g (3 cups) basil, plus more to serve
50ml (3 tbsp) olive oil
½ garlic clove
Finely grated zest and juice of ½ lemon

1. Make the *piperade* (see page 65) and spread it in a round ovenproof serving dish.

2. Preheat the oven to 200°C fan (425°F).

3. Now for the ratatouille, and the more time you take at this stage, the more impressive your finished dish will look. Slice the courgettes, aubergine and tomatoes into 5mm (¼ inch) slices. Leave them all lined up on your chopping board, then alternate placing the vegetables on top of the *piperade*, in a circular shape. Once your piece of veggie art is complete, drizzle with olive oil and sprinkle with salt and pepper. Cover with a lid or foil.

4. Bake for 20 minutes, covered, then remove the lid or foil and place it back in the oven for another 20 minutes.

5. Your ratatouille is ready and very delicious at this stage if you want to dive in. I just think the *pistou* gives a herby punch which helps elevate the dish. So, while the ratatouille is in the oven, place the basil in a blender with the oil and blend until smooth, then grate in the garlic and pulse-blend briefly. Finish with the lemon zest and juice, then scatter your ratatouille with basil and serve the *pistou* on the side, or generously spoon it over the dish, if you prefer.

Fennel à la grecque, crème fraîche, dill

This recipe takes a classic cooking technique to what I think is an underused vegetable. Fennel is great shaved raw and mixed through salads, yes, but slow-cooking – not often associated with the bulb – is my favourite way to enjoy it. The dish makes the perfect side to accompany some simply grilled chicken or seafood, or the gentle aniseed background flavour also makes it a no-brainer with any type of fish.

———— • ————

Cooking in a grecque *is similar to gently cooking and pickling a vegetable: water is flavoured with aromats, white wine, vinegar and olive oil. It's a common method in Greece, hence 'in the Greek style'. As with pickling, the longer the vegetable has in the liquor, the better. You can cook the fennel up to a week in advance, so it's a good one to get organised with. If you have a jar of the fennel in its cooking liquid in the fridge, it is also great sliced up cold in salad, or mixed through couscous.*

EASY

~

Prep time 20 minutes, plus cooling

Cooking time 45 minutes

Serves 4 as a side dish

~

For the fennel

50g (¼ cup) caster sugar

8 black peppercorns

1 tsp coriander seeds

1 thyme sprig

1 tarragon sprig

400ml (1⅔ cups) water

100ml (7 tbsp) olive oil, plus more to sear the fennel

100ml (7 tbsp) white wine

100ml (7 tbsp) white wine vinegar

6g (1 tsp) salt

2 fennel bulbs

Lemon wedges, to serve (optional)

For the dressing

150g (⅔ cup) crème fraîche

50g (3 tbsp plus 1 tsp) Dijon mustard

10g (4 tsp) chopped dill, plus more (optional) to serve

Sea salt flakes and fresh-cracked black pepper

1. Place all the ingredients for the fennel, except the fennel itself, in a large saucepan, big enough to hold the liquid and your fennel wedges. Bring to the boil and simmer for 2 minutes.

2. Meanwhile, remove the outermost layer from each fennel bulb and cut each in half vertically, then cut each half into 3 even wedges, with the root attached at the base of each to hold it together. Put the fennel in the simmering liquid and gently simmer for 20–30 minutes, or until tender.

3. Once a knife easily pieces the flesh, turn the temperature off and leave the fennel to cool down in the cooking liquid. This can be done up to 1 week in advance.

4. It couldn't be easier to make the dressing: just mix everything together, season up and check. It should pack a punch, so prepare for a little Dijon fieriness.

5. Take the cooled fennel out of the *grecque* liquor and leave on a piece of kitchen paper to dry.

6. In a large frying pan over a high heat, add a little oil and your fennel wedges on a flat cut side. Evenly caramelise all over, then finish with sea salt flakes.

7. Put the dill dressing on a large sharing platter and top with the roasted fennel, or dollop the dressing over the fennel if you prefer. Chef it up with dill sprigs and lemon wedges, if you're eating this with fish.

Chicory salad, capers, parsley

The punch of bitter chicory wedges, Dijon-spiked red wine vinaigrette and capers makes this salad the perfect accompaniment to fatty and rich foods, such as a charcuterie plate. I would also pick this over a green salad for cutting the richness of something like a Beef Bourguignon (see page 154), as the chicory wedges are much more robust, so the heat of the food takes a little longer to wilt the leaves.

———— • ————

All I have to say here is that you get the best results by dressing the chicory wedges heavily with vinaigrette. As the chicory is cut into wedges rather than individual leaves, it's harder to evenly distribute the dressing, so the more the merrier!

EASY

~

Prep time 10 minutes

Serves 6 as a side dish

~

For the dressing

40g (2½ tbsp) Dijon mustard

30ml (2 tbsp) red wine vinegar

½ small garlic clove, crushed or finely grated

180ml (¾ cup) rapeseed oil, or other good-quality vegetable oil

Juice of ¼ lemon

Sea salt flakes and fresh-cracked black pepper

For the salad

3 heads of red chicory, cut into wedges

3 heads of white chicory, cut into wedges

10g (1 tbsp) shallot, finely chopped (about ½)

20g (4 tsp) parsley leaves, chopped

50g (5 tbsp) brined capers, rinsed

1. Roll a tea towel into a tight rope, place on your worktop in a small circle and sit a mixing bowl inside this. It will stop the bowl from moving, so you can add your oil without having to hold the bowl steady.

2. Put the Dijon, vinegar and garlic in the bowl, whisk to combine, then slowly stream in the oil, whisking all the while, to make the dressing. Finish with seasoning and the lemon juice. Store in a squeezy bottle in the fridge to make dressing the leaves easier.

3. Dress the chicory wedges with plenty of dressing, add the shallot, parsley and capers, then toss with your hands until every leaf is evenly coated. Put on a large platter and finish with plenty of cracked black pepper.

For a photograph, see pages 156–157.

Green salad

Such a simple recipe, but I had to include this as it accompanies so many of my meals when I'm cooking at home. Crisp lettuce with a simple vinaigrette really is the perfect side dish for almost everything, from a simple Omelette all the way to a rich *Tartiflette* or Lobster Thermidor (see pages 77, 175 and 102). Salad leaves are abundant in my garden at the right time of year: you pick them, and, before you know it, you have a new crop to harvest. I make this dressing in big batches, so it's always in the fridge. Double or triple the recipe, depending on how much salad you eat each week!

———— • ————

Approach making the vinaigrette like making a mayonnaise (see page 253), treating the Dijon as if it were the egg yolks. Slowly stream in the oil, constantly whisking: you want to make sure you're left with a thick emulsified dressing. If it splits and is too liquid, it won't coat the leaves properly. Add plenty of dressing and toss with your hands until every leaf is evenly coated, then serve quickly, as after about ten minutes the vinegar in the dressing will start to wilt the leaves and you'll lose that satisfying crunch.

EASY

~

Prep time 10 minutes

Serves 6 as a side dish

~

For the dressing

30g (2 tbsp) Dijon mustard

30ml (2 tbsp) white wine vinegar

½ small garlic clove, crushed or finely grated

180ml (¾ cup) rapeseed oil, or other good-quality vegetable oil

Juice of ¼ lemon

Sea salt flakes and fresh-cracked black pepper

For the salad

6 handfuls of leaves, washed and dried well and left whole

10g (1 tbsp) shallot, finely chopped (about ½)

5g (2 tsp) chopped chives

1. Roll a tea towel into a tight rope, place on your worktop in a small circle and sit a mixing bowl inside this. It will stop the bowl from moving, so you can add your oil without having to hold the bowl steady.

2. Put your Dijon, vinegar and garlic in the bowl, whisk to combine and slowly stream in the oil, whisking all the while, to make the dressing. Finish with the lemon juice and season well. Store in a squeezy bottle in the fridge, to make dressing the leaves easier.

3. Dress the washed, dried leaves with plenty of dressing, add the shallot and toss with your hands until every leaf is evenly coated. Put in a large bowl and sprinkle with chopped chives to finish.

For a photograph, see pages 104–105.

Radicchio, walnut, pear, Roquefort

This could be one of my favourite salad combinations. The Waldorf salad is a globally famous salad, originating in America, which this recipe is loosely based on. So you're probably wondering where the French bit comes in! I'll tell you: it comes in the shape of the ultimate blue cheese: Roquefort. This is one of the oldest known cheeses and is protected by European law. It is made from ewe's milk and is regarded as the king of cheeses. So, forget all I said just now about Waldorf salad, this combination is all about the Roquefort cheese and therefore is an absolute French classic!

———— • ————

Autumn is the time of year to be making this salad, when pears are at their best and wintry radicchio leaves are abundant. It's the sort of salad I want to eat with a nicely cooked steak or braised piece of beef and a large glass of red wine after a long dark day. But, if you want to skip the meat, roasted beetroots are a lovely addition to this salad and make it more of a complete meal.

EASY

~

Prep time 15 minutes
Cooking time 6 minutes
Serves 4

~

50g (½ cup) walnuts
1 head of radicchio
1 pear
200g (7oz) Roquefort cheese

For the dressing
1 egg yolk
35ml (2 tbsp plus 1 tsp) apple cider vinegar
30g (2 tbsp) Dijon mustard
125ml (½ cup) olive oil
25ml (1½ tbsp) water
Sea salt flakes and fresh-cracked black pepper

1. Preheat the oven to 180°C fan (400°F). Toast the walnuts on a small baking tray in the oven for 6 minutes. With a tea towel, rub the toasted nuts to remove some of the excess skins, then chop roughly, ready for sprinkling.

2. Roll a tea towel into a tight rope, place on your worktop in a small circle and sit a mixing bowl inside this. It will stop the bowl from moving, so you can add your oil without having to hold the bowl steady.

3. Put the egg yolk, vinegar and Dijon in the bowl, whisk to combine, then slowly stream in the oil, whisking all the time, to make the dressing. Finish with the splash of water, just enough to get the correct consistency, then season.

4. Cut the radicchio into quarters and remove the white core, then break it down into separate leaves, wash and dry. I like to leave the skin on my pear, but feel free to peel if you prefer, then cut into wedges, remove the core and slice thinly lengthways.

5. Dress the washed, dried leaves with plenty of dressing, add the sliced pear and toss with your hands until every leaf and pear wedge is evenly coated. Put in a large bowl and sprinkle with the toasted walnuts. Now crown your salad with the king of cheeses: crumble Roquefort all over the top and get the bowl in the middle of the table to be shared.

Globe artichoke, sauce ravigote

EASY

~

Prep time 20 minutes, plus cooling
Cooking time 55–70 minutes
Serves 4 as a starter

~

For the artichokes

150g (¾ cup) caster sugar

20 black peppercorns

3 tsp coriander seeds

3 thyme sprigs

3 tarragon sprigs

1.2 litres (5 cups) water

300ml (1¼ cups) white wine

300ml (1¼ cups) white wine vinegar

18g (3 tsp) sea salt flakes

4 globe artichokes

For the sauce ravigote

30g (2 tbsp) Dijon mustard

30ml (2 tbsp) white wine vinegar

¼ garlic clove

130ml (½ cup) rapeseed oil, or other good-quality vegetable oil

Juice of ¼ lemon

20g (2 tbsp) shallot, finely chopped (about 1 small)

20g (2 tbsp) brined capers, rinsed and chopped

20g (2 tbsp) cornichons, chopped

10g (4 tsp) mixed soft herb leaves, chopped (tarragon, chervil, parsley)

Sea salt flakes and fresh-cracked black pepper

If you haven't cooked or eaten a globe artichoke before, they can be a pretty daunting vegetable to attack. Prepping artichokes is still one of my least favourite jobs in the kitchen, hence why you'll find that prepared artichoke hearts appear on so few of my menus! This recipe, on the other hand, is a great gateway to globe artichokes, as it requires very little prep. The outer leaves are mostly inedible and would usually be removed before cooking, however in this instance they make useful vessels with which to scoop *ravigote*. Sauce ravigote is basically a tartare sauce bound with vinaigrette rather than mayonnaise, so it's slightly more acidic, making it a great match for fatty meats, as well as for vegetables such as artichokes.

——— • ———

Sorry if this tip is a little condescending, but I know my wife would appreciate guidance on how to eat a whole globe artichoke! To eat them, pull the leaves from the cooked artichokes one at a time, starting from the outside. At the base of each leaf there is a small piece of cooked artichoke flesh: dip this in the ravigote *sauce, and, using your teeth, scrape to remove the artichoke flesh and dressing. As you get closer to the centre of the artichoke, the crown is revealed and you'll be left with the full artichoke heart, which is the best bit!*

1. Place all the ingredients for the artichokes, except the artichokes themselves, in a large saucepan, big enough to hold the liquid and all 4 artichokes. Bring to the boil and simmer for 2 minutes. Cut the stalks off the artichokes so you have flat sides for them to sit on a plate later. Put them in the pan, cover with a lid and gently simmer for 45–60 minutes, depending on size. They are ready when a small sharp knife easily slips through the base of an artichoke into its heart.

2. Once cooked, remove from the liquid (reserve the liquid) and leave the artichokes to cool slightly. Prise open the centre of each artichoke and pull out some of the small centre leaves to reveal the hairy choke. Using your fingers or a spoon, you want to scrape this out. Now leave all the prepared artichokes in a container covered with some of the cooking liquid, to lightly pickle them.

3. To make the *ravigote*, mix the mustard, vinegar and garlic together in a blender. Slowly add the oil, with the blender running, until it's emulsified. Season with the lemon juice, salt and pepper, then mix in all the remaining ingredients by hand, or briefly pulse-blend, depending on what final texture you want.

4. For this dish, you want to serve the artichokes hot. If you need to reheat them, steam them, or place them in a saucepan with 1cm (½ inch) of boiling water and close the lid for a few minutes. Serve, with the *ravigote* on the side.

White asparagus, beurre blanc

As the cold winter months give way to spring, the most eagerly awaited seasonal delight is asparagus. White asparagus remains a bit of a mystery to us, but, while it requires a little more prep, it's well worth the effort; when you make this recipe, you'll see why it is so popular in mainland Europe. Slow-cooking with lemon and herbs gives it a delicate, almost-pickled quality, making it a perfect match for this classic sauce. The rich sauce is beautifully balanced by the asparagus's subtle acidity, so it makes a perfect seasonal starter.

———— • ————

Cook the asparagus slowly. The water should be very gently simmering, if at all: you want to see steam rising from the pan, with only a few small bubbles breaking the surface. The longer your asparagus has in the pan, the more it will soak up the flavours of your cooking liquid. Once almost cooked, leave it to cool in the liquid, for further flavour absorption. Cream is definitely not classic in a beurre blanc *and I'll get hunted down for suggesting it, but I find a glug helps stabilise the sauce and prevent it splitting.*

ELEVATED

~

Prep time 15 minutes, plus cooling

Cooking time 30 minutes

Serves 4 as a starter

~

For the asparagus

Large bunch of white asparagus

1 lemon, halved

75g (5 tbsp) butter, chopped

3 thyme sprigs

1 bay leaf

Sea salt flakes

For the beurre blanc

75g (scant ½ cup) shallots, finely chopped (about 3)

50ml (3 tbsp) white wine

50ml (3 tbsp) white wine vinegar

50ml (3 tbsp) double cream

200g (1½ sticks plus 1 tbsp) butter, chilled and chopped

10g (4 tsp) chives, chopped

1. Start by peeling the white asparagus: starting 2.5cm (1 inch) down from the tip, peel all the way to the base, rotating after each swipe of the peeler to leave none of the tough woody exterior attached. The woody base needs removing next; it's usually the last 2.5–5cm (1–2 inches) and can be found by snapping in your hands.

2. Put the peeled asparagus in a wide-based pan and barely cover with water, then add the lemon juice, the squeezed-out lemon shells and all the remaining ingredients for the asparagus. Slowly bring towards simmering, then cook for around 15 minutes before checking: once a knife easily pierces the flesh, take off the heat and leave the asparagus to cool down in the cooking liquid. To heat up before serving, just bring the pan back up to simmering.

3. To make the *beurre blanc*, put the shallots in a small pan over a medium heat with the wine and vinegar. Bring to the boil and reduce until the liquid has gone. Now add the cream and reduce until it, too, has almost completely gone.

4. Now turn the temperature right down and slowly whisk in the chopped butter, straight from the fridge, a few cubes at a time, making sure the sauce doesn't boil at any stage. Once all the butter has been emulsified, finish with the chopped chives and plate up with the asparagus while it is fresh. If you want to keep the sauce for a little while, just keep it somewhere warm to stop it from splitting.

Tomato salad, vierge dressing

A simple salad which relies fully on the quality of the ingredients. I would only make this salad in the summer, when the best tomatoes are in season. Go to your local farmers' market and seek out local heritage tomatoes which have been grown slowly. Not only do the different colours look amazing, but also the variety of textures and flavours is great. *Sauce vierge* is a classic French sauce in which tomatoes are usually cut into small dice as you would for a salsa, but for this salad I've taken those flavours and saved you some chopping... This is tomato salad aka chunky *sauce vierge*!

———— • ————

There is only one thing to mention with tomatoes, apart from the obvious fact that they must be ripe and ready to eat. When you eat a tomato, it must be at room temperature: a tomato from the fridge has absolutely no flavour! That's why a tomato you pick straight from the plant in a greenhouse tastes so sweet and full of flavour. Pull your tomatoes out of the fridge two hours early and dress them about ten minutes before you want to eat them; this gives the salt some time to macerate and intensify those tomato flavours.

EASY

~

Prep time 15 minutes, plus macerating

Cooking time 3 minutes

Serves 4

~

600g (1¼lbs) tomatoes, at room temperature (see tip, above)

Fresh-cracked black pepper

For the dressing

8 coriander seeds

10 fennel seeds

½ garlic clove, finely grated

Finely grated zest and juice of ½ lemon

100ml (7 tbsp) olive oil

5g (2 tsp) chopped basil leaves

3g (1 tsp) chopped parsley leaves

3g (1 tsp) chopped chervil, or more chopped parsley leaves

Sea salt flakes and freshly ground white pepper

1. Toast the coriander and fennel seeds in a dry pan over a medium heat. Once fragrant, take off the heat and crush in a mortar and pestle. Mix with all the other dressing ingredients, then check the seasoning.

2. Cut the tomatoes into random chunks of an even size, something about 5 x 4cm (2 x 1¾ inches) is good here. Season the tomatoes with all the dressing, sea salt flakes and black pepper, plate up, then leave to macerate for 10 minutes before serving.

For a photograph, see pages 130–131.

Green asparagus, sauce gribiche

Asparagus is undoubtedly the king of spring! The race to get this vegetable in the shops and on our plates happens each year, so do yourself a favour and avoid the ridiculous £15–20 bunches during the first week or so of the season; as the supply increases, the cost becomes a little less painful. It may be tempting to buy the cheaper supermarket asparagus grown all year round in Peru, but restrict yourself to the actual European season. English green asparagus is a real treat: carefully cooked, seasoned up with a little olive oil, lemon juice and salt, it's something I truly look forward to each year.

———— • ————

Gribiche is a basically a tartare sauce with added chopped boiled eggs, which I think is best suited to vegetables. When it comes to preparing the asparagus, snap each spear individually, as they are all woody in different places. In fancy restaurants, chefs waste their time removing the leafy scales from the spears of the asparagus: I suggest skipping this stage, just remove the woody ends and get cooking.

EASY

~

Prep time 20 minutes
Cooking time 15 minutes
Serves 4 as a starter

~

Bunch of green asparagus
30ml (2 tbsp) olive oil
Juice of ½ lemon
Chopped chives (optional), to serve

For the gribiche

1 egg
35g (scant ¼ cup) shallot, finely chopped (about 1 large)
20g (2 tbsp) cornichons, finely chopped
10g (1½ tbsp) Lilliput brined capers, rinsed and chopped
5g (2 tsp) chopped mint leaves
5g (2 tsp) chopped parsley leaves
5g (2 tsp) chopped tarragon leaves
Finely grated zest and juice of 1 lemon
120g (½ cup) mayonnaise (see page 253 for homemade)
Sea salt flakes and fresh-cracked black pepper

1. Start by cooking the egg. Place in a saucepan of boiling water for 10 minutes. Run under a cold tap to stop the cooking, then peel and finely chop.

2. In a bowl, mix all the ingredients for the *gribiche*, taste and add salt and pepper if required. Keep at room temperature to serve with the asparagus.

3. Put a saucepan of water generously seasoned with salt over a high heat and bring to the boil. Each asparagus spear shows you where it gets woody: they turn from vibrant green to white along their length from the tip down, then into a greyish colour. Snap the spear with your hands where the green stops.

4. When the water is rapidly boiling, add the asparagus spears for 2–3 minutes or until cooked. A small sharp knife should pierce the base of a spear, but meet just a little resistance, as you want them to be firm and hold their shape rather than bend; you don't want them overcooked. Drain well and season with the olive oil, lemon juice and salt.

5. Plate up and serve with a big dollop of *gribiche* sauce, sprinkled with chives, if you like.

For a photograph, see pages 142–143.

Spring cabbage, anchoïade, chilli

I can say with absolute confidence this dish will blow your mind... providing you like cabbage, chilli, garlic and anchovies, it is unbeatable! *Anchoïade* is a classic Provençal dip made by slowly cooking garlic in milk to mellow its flavour; this paste is then used to emulsify oil, anchovies and vinegar into an intense dressing. You'll find it in many restaurants across the south of France, served at the start of a meal as part of a crudité platter. I haven't been lucky enough to visit, but the most talked-about version is served at Club 55 in St Tropez. Though it's perfect with raw vegetables, *anchoïade* also marries amazingly with simply cooked vegetables, such as this cabbage.

———— • ————

This sauce keeps well in the fridge, so I tend to make bigger quantities and use it throughout the week. Try it with other vegetables, too: I love it over broccoli and Brussels sprouts at the right time of year. It's like an aïoli with the added umami hit of anchovies, so, as you can imagine, it's pretty great smeared over anything at all.

ELEVATED

~

Prep time 20 minutes, plus chilling
Cooking time 1 hour
Serves 4

~

For the anchoïade

80g (2¾oz) garlic cloves (about a whole large bulb/2 small bulbs)

175ml (¾ cup) water

215ml (¾ cup plus 2 tbsp) whole milk

15 good-quality anchovy fillets

5ml (1 tsp) good-quality white wine vinegar, ideally Chardonnay

5ml (1 tsp) lemon juice

40ml (3 tbsp) vegetable oil

For the cabbage

1 large spring cabbage, or 2 small

25ml (1½ tbsp) olive oil, plus more to season

Chilli flakes

Finely chopped chives

Croutons (see page 36)

Sea salt flakes and fresh-cracked black pepper

1. Ahead of time, make the garlic paste. Start by peeling the garlic cloves; if you're really lucky, you'll be able to find them pre-peeled like we get in the restaurant. Put them in a medium saucepan over a low heat with the measured water and milk and simmer very slowly until you have a thick paste; this can take up to 45 minutes. Once you have that thick paste, turn off the heat and leave to cool, then chill.

2. In a blender, mix the chilled garlic paste with the anchovies, vinegar and lemon juice. Slowly add the oil with the blender running as if you were making a mayonnaise, adding a little water if the *anchoïade* is too thick; it should have a similar consistency to tomato ketchup. This will keep in the fridge happily for more than a week if stored properly (I keep mine in a squeezy bottle).

3. Bring water to the boil in the base of a large steamer. Remove the large outer leaves from the cabbage(s), cut into quarters if you've sourced a large cabbage, or in half if they're smaller. Steam the cabbage(s) for around 6 minutes, or until almost cooked, cool, then place in the fridge to chill.

4. In a red-hot frying pan, or over a charcoal grill, colour the flat sides of the chilled cabbage in the oil. Once they are charred, season with a little more olive oil, salt and pepper. Dress the coloured cabbage with the *anchoïade* and top with chilli flakes, chives and croutons to serve.

SWEET

·

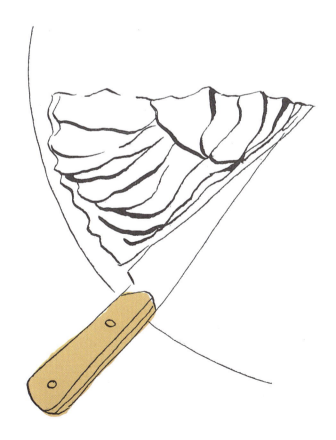

Chocolate mousse

For me, this is an absolute must in everyone's cooking repertoire. Who doesn't enjoy a smooth, airy chocolate mousse? It's a simple dessert with only a few ingredients, as with all the great French puds. It is also dairy-free, which is a massive bonus! The chocolate mousse recipe you may know that uses whipped cream is an American adaptation; the French egg-only classic results in a denser, richer texture and taste which lets the chocolate be the star, as it should be. Serve as it is, or push the boat out and top with Crème Chantilly (see page 218) and cherries dressed in kirsch, for Black Forest gateau vibes.

———— • ————

For the best results, use older eggs. As an egg gets older, the egg white becomes looser; while this is not what you want for poached eggs, for a mousse it's perfect. The looser egg whites have more elasticity, meaning they are able to stretch and incorporate air without breaking, and, if they are at room temperature, that will also help. I always give my bowl and utensils a quick wash before using them for whisking egg whites, as any fat will also stop the whites from aerating properly.

EASY

~

Prep time 15 minutes, plus 1–2 hours chilling

Cooking time 5 minutes

Serves 4

~

135g (4¾oz) 72 per cent cocoa solids chocolate, chopped, plus more to serve

85g (⅓ cup) egg yolks (4–5)

60g (⅓ cup) caster sugar, plus 25g (2 tbsp)

250g (1 cup) egg whites (7–8)

1. Set a heatproof bowl over a small pan of simmering water, make sure the inside of the bowl is completely dry, then add the chocolate and stir until fully melted. Leave to cool slightly.

2. Whisk the egg yolks with the 25g (2 tbsp) of sugar to ribbon stage (see page 275), using electric beaters or a stand mixer. Once thick and aerated, set aside.

3. Put the egg whites in a very clean, dry bowl and start to whisk with a clean whisk. Add the 60g (⅓ cup) sugar in 3 stages: at the start, middle and end of whisking. Whisk until you have stiff peaks and can hold the bowl upside down over your head without any mishap.

4. Pour the slightly cooled chocolate into the whisked egg yolks and mix well.

5. Add one-third of the egg white to lighten the mix; don't worry too much about knocking the air out of the mix at this stage. Now gently fold in the remaining two-thirds of the egg whites, in a figure of '8' motion.

6. Once fully combined, spoon the chocolate mousse into small individual serving dishes, or if you're planning on sharing, a large bowl. Set in the fridge for 1–2 hours, then grate over dark chocolate to serve.

Apple tarte fine

EASY

~

Prep time 30 minutes
Cooking time 1 hour
Serves 6

~

40g (3 tbsp) Demerara sugar, plus more to sprinkle

320g rectangular sheet of shop-bought all-butter puff pastry, about 30 × 25cm (14-oz sheet all-butter puff pastry, thawed if frozen, about 12 × 10 inches)

6 Pink Lady apples (see tip, right)

50g (3 tbsp) butter, melted

Apricot jam

For the crème Chantilly

250ml (1 cup) whipping cream

25g (¼ cup) icing sugar

¼ vanilla pod, split lengthways, seeds scraped out

Just like parents shouldn't have favourite children, while writing this book I've tried not to have favourite recipes. I love all the recipes in this section equally... just this one a little more equally, as it's easy to make and so delicious. *Tarte fine*, or 'thin tart', requires no lining of a tart ring, just a flat sheet of puff pastry topped with sliced apples, baked and glazed. Simples. Eat it while it's still warm with a whipped vanilla crème Chantilly. I've said the recipe is for six, but I've been known to eat an entire tart in a single sitting, so I'll let you be the judge. It counts towards your five-a-day, right?

———— • ————

The variety of apple is important here. I know they're expensive, but Pink Lady was the top performer in all my trials. It has a firm flesh which holds when baking and the perfect balance of sweetness and acidity. Peel, core and slice all the apples in one go; I use a small, serrated knife; it takes a little longer but will save you time in the long run, as the slices stay in order and so it makes building the tart easier. Dusting the base of the baking tray with Demerara sugar will give some extra crunch to your puff pastry and make it stay crisp for longer. The final step which gives the tart its elegant shine is called abricoter *(see page 272). Gently warm apricot jam and a little water and make sure you brush it over while the tart is still hot.*

1. Preheat the oven to 175°C fan (375°F). Line a baking sheet with baking paper, then sprinkle it with the Demerara sugar. Follow by laying on your sheet of puff pastry. Using a small knife, score a border 1cm (½ inch) from the outside of the pastry all the way around the rectangle. You'll want to keep the apple inside this line.

2. This really is such an easy recipe to put together, you'll just need some patience with the peeling and slicing of the apples! Peel an apple, and, using a corer, remove the centre where the pips are. Cut it in half through the centre so you're left with 2 half apples. (Or, if you don't have a corer, halve the apples first, then scoop out the seeds with a melon baller or sharp teaspoon.) Put the apple halves flat side down on a work surface and carefully slice each 1–2mm (¹⁄₁₆ inch) thick. Keep the apple slices together, so the halves still resemble a half apple once sliced. Repeat to prepare all the apples in the same way.

3. Starting at the top of the pastry, across a short side, you want to make a neat, slim row of sliced apples. To do this, take a half apple and slide the chopped slices out into a line over the pastry, standing up on their flat sides, curved sides uppermost. Repeat this process with parallel rows of fruit, until you have covered all the pastry. You want the apples to be standing up at this stage to achieve a thick layer of fruit, rather than laid down and flat (though they will be pressed a little later). Brush with the melted butter and sprinkle with Demerara sugar.

4. Bake in the hot oven for 35 minutes.

5. Remove the tart from the oven, place another sheet of baking paper on top, put another flat tray on top of the tart and press down gently. Put the tart back in the oven with the tray pressing on top and bake for a further 25 minutes.

6. Warm a few spoons of apricot jam in a small pan and brush over the top of the hot tart to glaze it and make it nice and shiny. Let cool slightly before portioning, but it's best enjoyed warm, so don't leave it too long.

7. Put all the ingredients for the crème Chantilly in a mixing bowl and whip to soft peaks. Serve with slices of the warm apple tart.

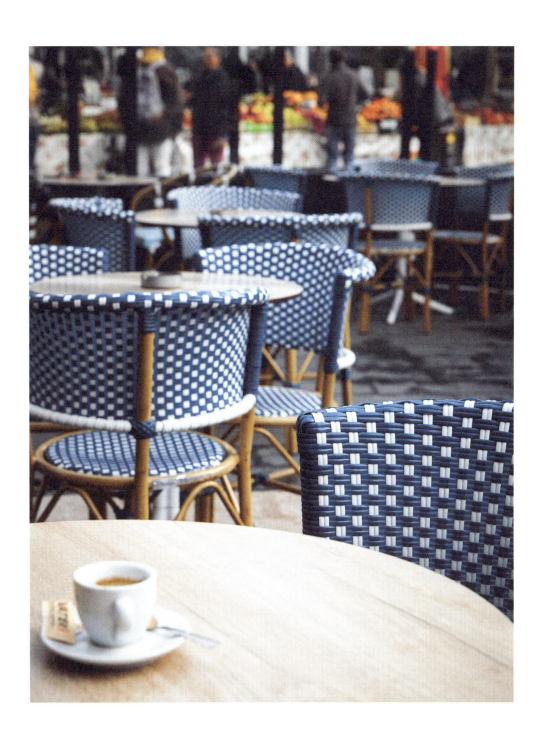

Crème brûlée

This could be one of the most talked-about French desserts of all time, a silky-smooth and rich vanilla custard which is just set, then topped with a thin pane of crunchy, dark, almost-bitter caramel. Everyone should have near enough all the ingredients to make this already kicking around, so there's no excuses! The pastry chef from a restaurant where I used to work introduced me to this recipe, which takes all the guesswork out of the cooking: the result is a perfect brûlée with that silky-smooth mouthfeel every time!

———— • ————

This dish is all about the balance of flavours: it should not be sickly sweet or taste only of vanilla, you should be able to taste the egg, too. The caramel should be taken as dark as you dare, as that brings bitterness to cut through the rich custard. And the amount of sugar in the custard is less than you're used to adding, so you'll just have to trust me. Cook the custard slowly and take it all the way to 88°C (190°F), then blend until silky-smooth and make sure it has ample time in the fridge to set. You can do this the day before you want it. The nice thing about making brûlée this way is that you can set it in any dish you like, it doesn't need to be ovenproof as it would with the traditional under-the-grill method.

EASY

~

Prep time 20 minutes, plus infusing and at least 2–3 hours chilling and cooling

Cooking time 10 minutes

Serves 4

~

* You will need a kitchen blowtorch and 4 ramekins, or other individual serving dishes.

560ml (2⅓ cups) double cream

1 vanilla pod, split lengthways and seeds scraped out

3 eggs

25g (2 tbsp) caster sugar

Demerara sugar, for the sugar crust

1. Put the cream, vanilla pod and seeds into a saucepan over a medium heat. Bring the cream to the stage just before boiling, take off the heat and leave to infuse for 20 minutes.

2. In a bowl, crack the eggs and add the caster sugar, then whisk until fully combined.

3. Put the infused cream back on the heat and bring back towards boiling. Slowly pour it over the egg mix, stirring as you go. Pour everything back into the pan and set over a low heat. Stirring with a spatula, cook until it reaches 88°C (190°F) on a probe thermometer. Take off the heat, pour through a sieve into a clean bowl and leave for 15 minutes.

4. Blend until very smooth. Pour into individual dishes and place into the fridge for 2–3 hours, or until set (the longer the better, so do this the day before, if you can).

5. When it comes to serving, sprinkle generously with Demerara sugar and caramelise using a kitchen blowtorch. You want to take the sugar as dark as you dare; it's the sweet-bitterness from the caramel which is key to this dish.

6. Leave to cool before serving, so the brûlée has time to cool and the caramel time to set rock-solid. Do not refrigerate though, as that would soften the sugar crust.

Raspberry soufflés

ELEVATED

~

Prep time 30 minutes, plus cooling

Cooking time 2 hours

Serves 4

~

* You will need 4 individual soufflé moulds, 9cm (3½ inches) in diameter and 7–8cm (2¾–3¼ inches) tall and a piping bag (optional).

For the rice pudding base

10g (2 tsp) butter

55g (¼ cup) pudding rice

250ml (1 cup) whole milk

250ml (1 cup) double cream

45g (scant ¼ cup) caster sugar

Pinch of salt

1 vanilla pod, split lengthways and seeds scraped out

For the soufflé

125g (1 cup) fresh raspberries, plus more if needed

100g (7 tbsp) egg whites, at room temperature (about 3)

40g (3 tbsp) caster sugar, plus more for the moulds

135g (½ cup plus 1 tbsp) Rice Pudding Base, at room temperature (see above)

Soft butter, for the moulds

Icing sugar, to dust

This is a recipe I first came across when training to be a chef and it has stuck with me ever since. A chef demo-ed it in our college lecture hall, without a set of scales, to show how foolproof the recipe is! More commonly, soufflé bases are made of a fruit purée or custard mix thickened with cornflour. This recipe is not only completely flour- and gluten-free, but combines two of my favourite things: rice pudding and soufflés. The rice pudding both stabilises the egg white and adds flavour. It's completely delicious and gives that moreish rice pudding flavour to a beautifully light fruit dessert. In my first role as a senior chef in London, we had a big VIP in for dinner who requested his favourite dessert: raspberry soufflé, of course. The pressure I felt to perfect it was immense, but thankfully this recipe didn't fail me and the VIP said it was one of the best soufflés he'd ever had.

———— • ————

The rice pudding base gives a very firm, stable soufflé which doesn't collapse quickly. Brushing the moulds with butter is important for a nice even rise. I double-butter my ramekins, just to make sure nothing is missed! If you have a little more rice pudding base than you need, it will hold in the fridge, just heat it up a little before using it again. Equally, I like eating this rice pudding purée as it is: I'm obsessed with rice pudding, and this purée, with a few raspberries on top, is a great midweek pud. If raspberry isn't your go-to flavour, substitute it with any fruit purée and this exact recipe will work just fine.

1. Start with the rice pudding base. Place a heavy-based ovenproof pan over a medium heat, add the butter and swirl the pan to melt it. Add the rice and cook for 1 minute. Add the milk, cream, sugar and salt, vanilla pod and seeds. Bring to the boil, then reduce the heat right down and cook at a bare simmer, stirring frequently, for 20 minutes, or until the mixture has thickened enough for the rice grains to remain suspended in it when stirred.

2. Meanwhile, preheat the oven to 110°C fan (265°F).

3. Cover the pan with a *cartouche* (see page 272), transfer to the oven and cook for 1½ hours, stirring every 15 minutes. Discard the vanilla pod, then leave to cool for 10 minutes. Transfer to a blender and blend to a smooth purée. Push this purée through a fine-meshed sieve, then cover and chill. Bring to room temperature, or warm very slightly, before use.

4. Press the fresh raspberries through a clean fine-meshed sieve. You need 100g (7 tbsp) of purée, so when you have that amount, set it aside.

5. When ready to bake, preheat the oven to 180°C fan (400°F).

6. Put the egg whites into a stand mixer fitted with a whisk attachment. Whisk at a high speed for 30 seconds. Add one-quarter of the caster sugar, then whisk for 30 seconds. Add the remaining caster sugar in 3 further batches in the same way, continuing to whisk until the whites form stiff peaks.

7. Place the slightly warm rice pudding base in a bowl, stir through the raspberry purée and mix well. Spoon one-quarter of the whisked whites into the raspberry purée mix and fold in until incorporated. Add the remaining whites and gently fold in a figure of '8' motion until you have a smooth and silky mix.

8. Prepare 4 individual soufflé moulds, each 9cm (3½ inches) in diameter and 7–8cm (2¾–3¼ inches) tall, by brushing them with soft butter, brushing it up from the bases to the rims with a pastry brush. Then coat with caster sugar, tapping out the excess. Repeat, if you like, to give a really thick coating. Spoon or pipe the soufflé mix into the prepared moulds, filling each to just above the rims. Run your pinched thumb and forefinger around each rim, to ensure the soufflés rise straight up.

9. Place the soufflés on a baking tray and place in the hot oven for 5 minutes, then turn the tray and leave for another 4 minutes or until well risen and golden. Remove the soufflés from the oven and dust with icing sugar to serve.

Cherry and almond clafoutis

My question is this: is a *clafoutis* a crustless tart or a cake? This recipe comes from a great pastry chef I worked with in Dubai more than ten years ago and I'm always making it at home. Everything goes into a single bowl and is mixed, then you add whatever fruit you have kicking around, depending on the time of year, and you have yourself a delicious treat. Cherry and almond is the traditional combination and the most delicious; when cherries are at their best in summer, you have to give this a go.

———— • ————

This is surprisingly easy to make this and it's pretty versatile. Yes, it's best with cherries in season, but the combinations of fruits and nuts you can use with this batter are endless. I make it throughout the year and change the fruit seasonally, so get creative and try some of your own combinations. Raspberry and ground and nibbed pistachios in spring, fig and hazelnut in autumn, pear and pecan in winter are just a handful of my favourites. Then, depending on whether it's cold or hot outside, I either cover with hot crème anglaise, cool cream, or top with scoops of vanilla ice cream.

EASY

~

Prep time 10 minutes, plus cooling
Cooking time 25–45 minutes
Serves 4–6

~

* You will need a 23cm (9 inch) diameter nonstick baking dish, about 3cm (1½ inches) deep, or 4–6 individual 300ml (10-oz) dishes.

60g (4 tbsp) butter, plus more for the dish

15g (2 tbsp) custard powder, gluten-free, if needed

125ml (½ cup) whole milk

165g (¾ cup plus 1 tbsp) caster sugar

150g (5½oz) eggs (about 3)

70g (¾ cup) ground almonds

Any flour, for the dish, gluten-free if needed

250g (9oz) cherries, pitted

50g (½ cup) flaked almonds

Icing sugar, to dust

1. Start by making a *beurre noisette*. In a small saucepan over a medium-high heat, add the butter and cook until brown and smelling nutty. It will splutter before going quiet, which is when you need to watch it carefully. When it is a deep golden brown and smells of biscuits, pour into a small bowl and set aside to cool before making the batter. Measure it: you need 35g (1¼oz) for this recipe.

2. Preheat the oven to 170°C fan (375°F).

3. In a large bowl, mix the custard powder and the milk with a whisk. Next add the sugar and eggs and mix until fully incorporated, then add the ground almonds and cooled *beurre noisette*.

4. Butter and flour a 23cm (9 inch) diameter nonstick baking dish about 3cm (1½ inches) deep, or 4–6 individual 300ml (10-oz) volume dishes. Pour the batter into the prepared dish or dishes, evenly distribute the pitted cherries over and sprinkle evenly with flaked almonds.

5. Bake for around 20 minutes if you've gone for individual puddings, or 30–40 if you've baked a large sharing *clafoutis*. The finished *clafoutis* should be golden brown, risen in the centre and firm to the touch.

Profiteroles with chocolate sauce

EASY

~

Prep time 25 minutes, plus cooling
Cooking time 40–45 minutes
Makes 18 choux buns / Serves 4
(or 2 if you're feeling greedy)

~

* You will need a piping bag.

For the choux pastry

50g (3 tbsp plus 1 tsp) butter
50ml (3 tbsp plus 1 tsp) whole milk
50ml (3 tbsp plus 1 tsp) water
5g (1 tsp) caster sugar
Pinch of salt
100g (3/4 cup plus 1 tbsp) plain flour
2 eggs, plus more if needed

For the cream

250ml (1 cup) whipping cream
25g (1/4 cup) icing sugar
1/4 vanilla pod, split lengthways and
seeds scraped out

For the sauce

25ml (1 1/2 tbsp) water
25g (2 tbsp) caster sugar
120ml (1/2 cup) whipping cream
100g (3 1/2 oz) 70 per cent cocoa solids
chocolate, chopped

Sunday lunch round at Nan's used be a regular occurrence, and hands down it is still the best roast dinner I've had. But it was not only the roast itself that was so special; dessert was also a complete revelation. There were always a minimum of three puddings, two homemade and one shop-bought for the fussy eaters. Nine times out of ten, the shop-bought choice was profiteroles piled high, with a cold, set chocolate sauce. I remember picking at these as a young boy, eating my big bowl of apple crumble with a few profiteroles on top. (As they were so small, they were easy to swipe without Mum noticing I'd taken another.) I was so impressed by the shop-bought profiteroles... just imagine if my nan had used this recipe to make her own and covered them with a warm, glossy chocolate sauce.

——— • ———

I would recommend making a double or triple recipe of the choux buns. In restaurants, it is regular practice to bake choux pastry from frozen, and there's no reason you shouldn't do the same at home. Make the mix and pipe it on to flat trays, put the trays in the freezer, and, once they are hard, knock them off the tray into a sealed container. Now you have choux ready to go whenever you need, even if it's just for a quick midweek pudding for two of you. Tray the frozen choux up and bake and fill as normal. As always, though, don't give in to temptation: keep that oven door closed for the whole time they are baking!

1. Start with the choux buns, so they have time to bake and cool while you are preparing the filling and chocolate sauce. Place a saucepan over a medium heat, add the butter, milk, measured water, sugar and salt and bring to the boil. Once it is boiling, add the flour, then mix well over a medium-low heat for 6–8 minutes, constantly stirring with a wooden spoon. Put into a bowl and leave to cool slightly.

2. Add the eggs one at a time, and, using the wooden spoon, beat until fully combined. Once both eggs have been added, the mixture should have a spooning consistency: this means it holds its shape, but when you take a spoonful and tap the spoon on the side of the bowl, the mix falls off. If the mix is too thick, add a little more egg. Place in a piping bag.

3. If you are planning to bake these straight away, preheat the oven to 170°C fan (375°F).

4. Put a small spot of choux mix on each corner of a baking sheet and line with baking paper; the mix will stop the paper from flying off in the oven. Pipe the mix with at least a 3cm (1¼ inch) gap between each profiterole; you're aiming for each to be slightly bigger than a £2 coin. Freeze them now, if you want (see recipe introduction), or proceed to bake them now.

5. Bake the choux buns for 25–30 minutes until firm and golden. Don't open the oven door while they're baking! Take out of the oven and leave to cool.

6. For the crème Chantilly filling, put all the ingredients into a bowl and whip together until you have soft peaks. Spoon into a piping bag, then make a small hole in the base of each cold profiterole and fill with the cream. Alternatively, cut the buns in half to fill them, if you want the cream on show.

7. Leave the chocolate sauce until you are ready to serve, as you want to be pouring this warm over your choux buns! Bring the measured water, sugar and cream to the boil. Put the chocolate in a heatproof bowl. Pour the hot water and cream mix over the chocolate and mix until the chocolate has melted. Pour generously over the top of your profiteroles. (Or over fresh strawberries, or directly into your mouth, this chocolate sauce is a winner over everything...)

Crème caramel

This velvety set custard, infused with vanilla, with its rich, dark, caramel syrup, balances indulgence and lightness and is surprisingly easy to make, so it's one of France's most popular desserts. It's a dish I first came across long before I appreciated what I was eating, and no, it wasn't this luxurious version... It came in a plastic pot with a tag on the bottom which, when you pulled, as if by magic slipped out of its packaging on to your plate. Although the flavours were not memorable, I remember the silky mouthfeel and always try to replicate it. Here, I've used a mix of milk and whipping cream, for the perfect texture. You can use vanilla extract instead of pods, but it won't have quite the same special flavour. This is a great make-ahead recipe and will sit happily in the fridge for a few days.

—— • ——

There are two main points to consider when making crème caramel: first, the colour of the caramel must be a deep brown: too light and it will taste merely sweet with no caramel flavour. Second, the egg mixture must be cooked until just set; it still needs to have a wobble, otherwise you'll lose that magical melt-in-the-mouth texture.

EASY

~

Prep time 10 minutes, plus at least 2 hours chilling

Cooking time 50 minutes

Serves 4

~

* You will need 4 small ramekins, each 9 x 5cm (3¹/₂ x 2 inches).

140g (²/₃ cup plus 1 tbsp) caster sugar

20ml (4 tsp) hot water

2 eggs, plus 1 egg yolk

200ml (³/₄ cup plus 1 tbsp) whole milk

100ml (7 tbsp) whipping cream

2 vanilla pods, split lengthways and seeds scraped out, or 2 tsp vanilla extract (see recipe introduction)

1. Preheat the oven to 130°C fan (300°F).

2. Start by making caramel. Have a bowl (or sink) of cold water to hand. Put 100g (¹/₂ cup) of the sugar in a heavy-based saucepan in an even layer. Add the measured hot water and allow the sugar to absorb it for a few minutes, then set over a medium heat and leave to dissolve. You can help it along by shaking the pan, but do not stir. Once a syrup forms, it will turn golden and then to a rich caramel colour. To stop the cooking, place the base of the pan in the bowl (or sink) of cold water. Divide it between 4 ramekins, each 9 × 5cm (3¹/₂ × 2 inches), then place in a roasting tin.

3. Whisk the eggs, yolk and remaining 40g (3 tbsp) of sugar in a bowl. Bring the milk, cream, vanilla seeds and pods, if using, to the boil in a saucepan, then pour slowly over the egg mix, whisking all the time. Pass through a sieve into each ramekin. Add the vanilla extract, if using.

4. Place the roasting tin in the oven and fill with enough boiling water to come halfway up each ramekin. Bake for 35 minutes, or until just cooked and still wobbling.

5. Cool, then chill for at least 2 hours, or overnight. Serve in the ramekins, or run a knife around each, turn out on to a plate with a rim and watch the caramel lakes spread out.

Hazelnut Paris-Brest

ELEVATED

~

**Prep time 30 minutes, plus chilling
and cooling**

Cooking time 55–60 minutes

Serves 6–8

~

** You will need 2 piping bags, 1 fitted
with a star nozzle.*

For the crème pâtissière

160ml (⅔ cup) whole milk

160ml (⅔ cup) whipping cream

1 vanilla pod, split lengthways and
seeds scraped out

75g (¼ cup plus 1 tbsp) caster sugar

25g (3 tbsp) cornflour (cornstarch)

65g (¼ cup) egg yolk (3–4)

25g (2 tbsp) butter, chopped

For the crème mousseline

150g (1 stick plus 1 tbsp) softened
butter

150g (⅔ cup) hazelnut praline paste
(bought online)

500g (2 cups) Crème Pâtissière
(see above)

For the pastry

75g (5 tbsp) butter

75ml (5 tbsp) whole milk

75ml (5 tbsp) water

10g (2 tsp) caster sugar

Pinch of salt

150g (1 cup plus 2 tbsp) plain flour

3 eggs, plus more if needed

50g (½ cup) flaked or sliced
hazelnuts (if you can't find them,
use flaked almonds)

Icing sugar, to dust

Another addition to the large family of French choux desserts, Paris-Brest is a wheel-shaped dessert filled with a hazelnut cream. The pudding was created by a French pastry chef in 1910 and named after a bike race which is 1,200km (750 miles) long, travelling from Paris to Brest. *Crème mousseline* is the traditional filling; it's a step further than the Crème Chantilly you might find in an éclair or profiterole (see page 230), but it's certainly worth it. If you like this hazelnut cream filling, try the same recipe with any praline paste: almond or pistachio are my favourites. It also makes for a great filling if you want to elevate your profiteroles or éclairs!

———— • ————

If the thought of making one giant Paris-Brest is slightly daunting, you can always pipe small individual rings, which are also nice for a dinner party, just bake them for 10 minutes less. If you do opt for the smaller rings, as is the case with the profiteroles you could also make extra mix, pipe and freeze them, then bake whenever you want them. A tip for the perfect circles when piping the choux: take a dish of the size of circle you want to pipe, place it on the baking paper and draw around it using a marker pen. Make sure you don't forget to flip the baking paper, so the circle you drew is on the opposite side to the choux you are piping. I've make that mistake before! And yes, you are left with a dark ring of ink on the base of your Paris-Brest...

1. Start with the *crème pâtissière*. Bring the milk, cream and vanilla pod and seeds to the boil. In a separate bowl, whisk together your sugar and cornflour, add the egg yolks and mix well. Pour half the hot vanilla milk over the egg yolk mixture, stirring all the time, then return the egg yolk mix to the pan with the remaining milk and cook, gently simmering and continually stirring, until the *crème pâtissière* is thick.

2. Leave to cool to around 50°C (122°F) on a probe thermometer before beating in the butter until smooth. Cover and place in the fridge to chill.

3. To finish the *crème mousseline*, whisk the softened butter in a bowl with electric beaters until light and fluffy, then whisk in the praline paste and finally whisk in the chilled *crème pâtissière*. Spoon the *mousseline* into a piping bag fitted with a star nozzle and put it into the fridge until you're ready to build the Paris-Brest.

4. When you're ready to make the choux pastry, preheat the oven to 170°C fan (375°F).

5. Place a saucepan over a medium heat, add the butter, milk, measured water, sugar and salt and bring to the boil. Once boiling, add the flour and mix well over a medium-low heat for 6–8 minutes, constantly stirring. Transfer this mix to a bowl and leave to cool slightly.

6. Add the eggs one at a time, using a wooden spoon to beat until fully combined. Once the eggs have been added, the mixture should have a spooning consistency: this means it holds its shape, but when you take a spoonful and tap the spoon on the side of the bowl, the mix falls off. If it is too thick, add a little more egg. Place in a piping bag and cut the end off to give you an opening of 1.5cm (5/8 inch).

7. Put a small spot of choux mix on each corner of a flat baking sheet and line it with baking paper. This will stop the paper from flying off in the oven. Pipe the mix in a large ring shape about 20cm (8 inches) in diameter, then pipe another ring on the inside of your first ring to make it thicker. Finally, finish by piping a third ring on top of the 2 you have just piped to make it taller. Sprinkle with the flaked hazelnuts.

8. Bake for 35–40 minutes. (Don't open the oven door while baking!) Take out of the oven and leave to cool.

9. Once the Paris-Brest has fully cooled, cut in half and pipe on your *crème mousseline* filling, spiralling your way around the ring. Put the top on your Paris-Brest and dust with icing sugar before serving.

Chocolate fondant

This rich, gooey chocolate dessert is pure melt-in-the-mouth decadence. You won't believe that it only needs four simple ingredients most will have kicking around their kitchen... or even that mine's completely gluten-free! When I have friends over for dinner, this is my go-to recipe; the melting texture and liquid centre make anyone smile. It's easy to do, but always impresses people when you serve a perfect fondant. Made in advance, this mix will sit happily in the fridge for a few days, just chuck them in a hot oven when you're ready.

———— • ————

It may take a couple of trial runs to perfect this (if it does, you're lucky, as a failed attempt means eating a lot of hot chocolate cake to hide the evidence). The exact timings will depend on your oven and dish size, but once you have it nailed, it's foolproof. I know after exactly eleven minutes in my oven, with a minute's rest, the fondants are perfect every time. Instead of serving these with vanilla ice cream, I like to serve my fondants with a slice of Viennetta; the crunchy chocolate running through it is pretty unbeatable, you've got to try it! (Trust me, you'll be telling everyone about this dessert – and life – hack!)

EASY

~

Prep time 10 minutes, plus chilling
Cooking time 15 minutes
Serves 4

~

* You will need 4 x 200–225ml (7–8fl oz) volume individual pudding basins or ramekins.

150g (5½oz) 70 per cent cocoa solids chocolate, chopped

120g (1 stick) butter, chopped, plus more soft butter for the moulds

4 eggs

120g (⅔ cup) caster sugar

Flour, to dust, gluten-free if needed

1. Place a small saucepan over a medium-high heat with 2.5cm (1 inch) of water in the base, bring to the boil, then reduce the heat to a simmer. Put a heatproof bowl over the simmering water and add the chocolate and butter, melting them gently over the bain marie. Once melted, remove from the heat.

2. Either using electric beaters in a separate bowl, or a stand mixer, whisk together the eggs and sugar until thick. This should take around 3 minutes: the mix should be light and airy, with the consistency of cake batter.

3. Combine the slightly cooled chocolate mix with the whisked eggs, using a wooden spoon or spatula, until fully combined. This mix now needs to be completely chilled before being baked. Pour into a clean bowl, cover and leave to chill for a couple of hours.

4. Preheat the oven to 170°C fan (375°F).

5. Rub 4 × 200–225ml (7–8fl oz) individual pudding basins or ramekins with soft butter and dust with flour, knock off the excess flour, then add your mix. Fill each two-thirds full with the chocolate mix and bake for 10–12 minutes. The finished fondants will have a firm, cake-like exterior and a soft centre with a slight wobble. Leave them to rest in the moulds for a minute before turning out to serve.

Tarte Tatin

ELEVATED

~

Prep time 20 minutes, plus drying, cooling, chilling and standing

Cooking time 40–50 minutes

Serves 4–6

~

* You will need a nonstick ovenproof pan with a diameter of about 20cm (8 inches).

6 Pink Lady apples (probably, but get 8 just in case)

500g shop-bought all-butter puff pastry block (14-oz sheet all-butter puff pastry, thawed if frozen)

100g (7 tbsp) soft butter, chopped

100g (½ cup) caster sugar

1 cinnamon stick

2–3 star anise

Everyone, I suspect, has at least heard of tarte Tatin, whether they've tried it or not. It's a tart that is baked upside down. While the pastry is cooking and crisping on top, the fruits are slowly caramelising underneath, protected from the harsh heat of the oven by the pastry. Apple is the most famous Tatin, and rightly so. I have experimented with everything from pear to fig to beetroot, but apple will always wear the crown. You could whip up a Crème Chantilly (see page 218) spiked with Cognac to go with it, but I prefer an ice cream with Tatin; vanilla is my favourite, but something spiced, alcoholic or nut-flavoured would be great too. Try rum and raisin, cinnamon or pistachio ice creams... in my next book I'll give you all those recipes, but for now, save yourself a job and head to the shops.

———— • ————

In many tarte Tatin recipes, you make the caramel in the base of the pan first, then put the fruit on top. With a fair amount of trial and error, I have found that attractively balancing apples on top of a sheet of hard caramel is near impossible. Instead, I put the soft butter and caster sugar in the pan first. This gives you a nice soft base to push your apples into, so they stand strong. With this method, you're forced to cook the caramel in the pan with the apples, which is a good way to make sure your apples poach and soak up maximum caramel! Keep an eye on the colour of the caramel through the slit in the centre of the pastry: dare to go dark! If your caramel is too blonde at the first stage, your finished tarte won't have that enticing caramelised brown colour.

1. Peel the apples, cut in half and remove the cores. Leave them to dry on a tray for around an hour. Don't worry about the apples discolouring, you won't be able to tell in the final result.

2. Roll out the pastry to the thickness of a £1 coin (about 1/8 inch) and cut a circle from it: the circle should be 5cm (2 inches) larger in diameter than the pan you are using. (In this case, about 25cm / 10 inches.) Prick the pastry circle all over with a fork.

3. Find a clean nonstick ovenproof pan with a diameter of around 20cm (8 inches). Add the soft butter and caster sugar to the base of the pan, spreading both out into an even layer, then place your spices on top, with the cinnamon in the centre. Working around the edge of the pan, stand your apples up, packing them all in and making sure the curved edges are all facing the same way. Push your apples into the butter and sugar as you go, so they stand strong.

4. Place the disc of pastry over the pan of apples and tuck the edges right down: don't try to do this too perfectly, as squished, overlapped puff pastry will give those nice crispy bits of puff around the outside of your tart. Just make sure they're tucked in nicely and try and get the pastry to touch the base of the pan. Cut a 2cm (3/4 inch) slit in the centre of the pastry, so you can peek at the cooking caramel in the next stage.

5. Preheat the oven to 180°C fan (400°F).

6. Put the pan over a high heat and watch the sugar. As it starts to caramelise around the side of the pan, gently shake the pan to mix the caramel and get an even colour. This should take at least 5 minutes but can take up to 10; keep rolling the caramel round the pan. You want to take this towards the darker end of the caramel spectrum: when the colour of the caramel in the middle of the pan – which you see through your peep hole – and the colour on the outside match, it is ready.

7. Bake in the hot oven for 40–50 minutes, until the pastry is golden brown, cooked thoroughly and slightly puffed. Leave for 5 minutes to stand before turning out.

8. Put a serving plate over the top of the pan, quickly and confidently turn both, so the tarte is on the plate, then carefully remove the pan from the top. You should be left with your perfect Tatin sitting on the plate.

BASICS

·

Vinaigrette

My go-to salad dressing: punchy and very moreish. I can't stop eating crisp salad leaves that have been dressed with this vinaigrette.

Prep time 5 minutes
Makes about 480ml (2 cups)

~

60g (¼ cup) Dijon mustard
60ml (¼ cup) white wine vinegar
½ small garlic clove, finely grated
Juice of ¼ lemon
360ml (1½ cups) rapeseed oil, or other good-quality vegetable oil
Sea salt flakes and fresh-cracked black pepper

1. This is a little bit like making a mayonnaise. Roll a tea towel into a tight rope, place on your worktop in a small circle and sit your mixing bowl inside this. It will stop the bowl from moving, so you can add your oil and whisk it in without having to hold the bowl steady.

2. In your bowl, start by whisking your Dijon, vinegar, garlic, seasoning and lemon juice. Slowly stream in your oil, still whisking, until you have a thick finished dressing. (Alternatively, add everything to a jam jar and shake well to emulsify.) Check the seasoning and serve.

Mayonnaise

Although there is an undeniable convenience to opening a jar of mayonnaise, hand-whisked mayonnaise is surprisingly easy to make. Seasoned heavily with Dijon mustard and lemon juice, the homemade version is also far more delicious.

Prep time 5 minutes
Makes about 200g (scant 1 cup)

~

2 egg yolks
20ml (4 tsp) white wine vinegar
1 tbsp Dijon mustard
175ml (¾ cup) rapeseed oil, or other good-quality vegetable oil
Juice of up to ¼ lemon, if needed
Sea salt flakes and fresh-cracked black pepper

1. Roll a tea towel into a tight rope, place on your worktop in a small circle and sit your mixing bowl inside this. It will stop the bowl from moving, so you can add your oil and whisk it in without having to hold the bowl steady.

2. Put your egg yolks, vinegar and Dijon in the bowl and whisk for 30 seconds to combine. Slowly stream your oil into the egg yolk mixture, still whisking continuously. As the mayonnaise begins to thicken, you can add the oil a little more quickly. If your mayonnaise gets too thick, add a little of your lemon juice to loosen the mayo, then finish adding your oil. Check the seasoning and serve.

For a photograph, see page 83.

Confit garlic

As you know, the French love garlic. I always keep a jar of confit garlic in my fridge, as it's a great way of adding a subtle garlicky flavour to your food. Drop it into a sauce or dressing. Spread it over grilled bread. Blend it into a delicious aïoli or tapenade. It takes a little while to cook, but will sit happily in the fridge for up to two months.

Prep time 10 minutes

Cooking time 45–60 minutes

Makes about 40 cloves (or enough for 2 months, if you use it as much as me)

~

4 garlic bulbs
Olive oil
6 thyme sprigs
1 bay leaf

1. Preheat the oven to 160°C fan (350°F).

2. Start by breaking down the garlic bulbs into cloves and peeling them. If you're lucky, you'll find some peeled garlic cloves sold somewhere, that's how we buy it at the restaurant! Choose an oven dish just big enough for the garlic cloves, then tip them in and cover completely with oil. Add your thyme and bay and submerge them in the oil, too.

3. Place in the oven and bake until the garlic cloves are soft, fragrant and lightly browned, but still holding their shape, 45–60 minutes. Remove from the oven and let cool to room temperature, then store in an airtight container in the fridge. If the garlic is completely covered with oil, it will keep in there for 2 months.

Béchamel

White sauce: one of the foundational mother sauces (see page 274) from which many others are made.

Prep time 5 minutes, plus infusing
Cooking time 10 minutes
Makes about 500ml (2 cups)

~

450ml (1¾ cups plus 2 tbsp) whole milk
½ onion
1 thyme sprig
⅕ nutmeg, freshly grated
5 cracks of black pepper
50g (3 tbsp) butter
40g (3 tbsp plus 1 tsp) plain flour
Sea salt flakes

1. For the milk infusion, put your milk and aromats (onion, thyme, nutmeg and black pepper) in a saucepan and slowly bring to the boil. Take off the heat, cover and leave to infuse for 10–20 minutes, then strain. You should be left with 400ml (1⅔ cups).

2. Melt the butter in a small pan over a medium heat, then add your flour. Cook the roux for around 3 minutes, stirring. It will be foaming and white. Once it turns slightly brown, reduce the heat and start slowly adding the milk.

3. Add the milk a ladle at a time, mixing after each addition until fully incorporated. Once you've added around half the milk, start adding 2 ladles at a time. Check the seasoning and correct with salt. If you're not using it immediately, transfer to a bowl and cover with clingfilm, directly touching the top of the béchamel to stop a skin forming. When cool, store in the fridge. It keeps for a couple of days.

Mornay sauce

One of the derivatives of béchamel, I've just had to include this as I use it so much, for a midweek lasagne, cauliflower cheese on Sunday or a cheeky brunch Croque Madame (see page 71).

Prep time 10 minutes
Cooking time 10 minutes
Makes about 500ml (2 cups)

~

40g (3 tbsp) butter
35g (3 tbsp) plain flour
300ml (1¼ cups) whole milk
Freshly grated nutmeg
150g (1½ cups) Gruyère, grated
1 egg yolk
Sea salt flakes and fresh-cracked black pepper

1. In a small pan over a medium heat, melt your butter, then add your flour. Cook the roux for around 3 minutes, stirring constantly. Once you see the colour start to turn slightly brown, reduce the heat and start adding milk.

2. Add the milk a ladle at a time, mixing after each addition until fully incorporated. Once you've added around half, start adding 2 ladles at a time. Adjust the seasoning to taste.

3. Add some nutmeg and the cheese and mix until smooth. Put it into a blender, add the egg yolk, then blend until smooth. If not using immediately, store as for béchamel.

Hollandaise sauce

Whisked egg yolks are enriched with melted butter and finished with lemon juice. Make sure your whisking arm is up to the challenge, as from start to finish it will be going for 10 minutes minimum to make this sauce, which is one of the French classic mother sauces (see page 274). Serve with eggs, fish and vegetables.

Prep time 5 minutes, plus cooling and chilling

Cooking time 15 minutes

Makes enough to serve 4

~

For the reduction

150ml (⅔ cup) white wine

150ml (⅔ cup) white wine vinegar

1 shallot, sliced

15 black peppercorns

3 thyme sprigs

For the clarified butter

240g (2 sticks) butter, chopped

For the sauce

3 egg yolks

40ml (2½ tbsp) Reduction (see above)

180g (¾ cup) Clarified Butter (see recipe method), warmed, or ghee

Lemon juice

Sea salt flakes and fresh-cracked black pepper

1. Put all the ingredients for the reduction in a saucepan and bring to the boil, then reduce the quantity by half. Leave to cool to room temperature, then store in the fridge for up to 2 months. The longer you leave the reduction to infuse, the better flavour it will have. Strain before use.

2. Now clarify the butter. Put the butter in a cold saucepan and slowly bring to the boil. Skim off the scum that rises to the top and leave the milk solids to sink to the bottom. The clear butter you're left with is what you want. Gently pour it off into a small bowl, leaving behind the milk solids (discard those). If clarifying butter for other recipes, reckon on losing about 25 per cent of its weight during the process.

3. Put the egg yolks in a heatproof bowl (I like to use a spherical-based bowl here), then whisk in the reduction. Set the bowl over a pan of gently simmering water and whisk the egg yolks and reduction; you want to keep doing this for 5–10 minutes until the egg is thick and aerated. Once cooked, you should be able to make a figure of '8' sign in the yolks and have the '8' stay visible for 8 seconds. If you have a probe thermometer, 80°C (176°F) is cooked.

4. As you would for a mayonnaise, slowly add the warmed clarified butter to the cooked yolks, starting with a very thin stream at first, whisking all the time. Finish with lemon juice, seasoning and add just a little warm water if the hollandaise is too thick.

For a photograph, see page 63.

Nage

A full-flavoured vegetable stock, often used for poaching delicate fish or vegetables in French cookery. At home, I use it for cooking rice, or as a chicken stock alternative when we aren't eating meat.

Prep time 10 minutes

Cooking time 45 minutes

Makes 2 litres (8 cups)

~

300g (10½oz) carrots, sliced

2 leeks, white parts only, sliced

100g (1 cup) celery, sliced

150g (scant 1½ cups) shallots (5–6), sliced

100g (1 cup) onion (about ½), sliced

2 garlic cloves, halved

250ml (1 cup) white wine

3 tbsp white wine vinegar

1 bouquet garni (see page 272)

10 white peppercorns

1. Put all the vegetables and garlic in a large pot and just-cover with cold water, then bring to the boil and simmer for 35 minutes.

2. Pour in the wine and vinegar, add the bouquet garni and white peppercorns and simmer for a final 10 minutes.

3. Strain the nage through a sieve into a bowl and leave to cool. Portion into storage containers or bags, then freeze for up to 3 months and use as required.

Fish stock

A proper well-made fish stock shows real skill and should set in the fridge in the same way as a gelatinous meat stock. Much quicker to cook than a meat stock, this only requires a 20-minute simmer: any longer and the bones and stock will turn bitter. Do not make fish stock with the bones of oily fish such as salmon or mackerel, as it will not taste pleasant!

Prep time 15 minutes, plus infusing
Cooking time 40 minutes
Makes 2 litres (16 cups)

~

1kg (2¼lb) fish bones, flat fish bones are best (ask your fishmonger)

Olive oil

1 tsp fennel seeds

6 white peppercorns

1 leek, white part only, sliced

½ celery stick, sliced

1 small onion, sliced

3 garlic cloves, halved

125ml (½ cup) white wine

2 bay leaves

Handful of herb stalks (parsley, dill, chervil or tarragon all work)

1 lemon, sliced

1. Cut your fish bones using sturdy kitchen scissors into roughly 5cm (2 inch) pieces and rinse them well.

2. Place a large saucepan over a medium heat and add some oil, followed by the fennel seeds, peppercorns and sliced vegetables and garlic, then sweat them (cook them slowly without colour). Once the vegetables are completely soft, add the fish bones and sweat slowly for another 10 minutes.

3. Add the wine and then enough water to just cover the bones and vegetables. Bring the stock to a gentle simmer: you do not want this to rapidly boil, or the stock will turn cloudy. Simmer for 20 minutes and skim any scum that rises to the top. Turn off the heat, add the herbs and lemon, then leave to infuse in the stock for a further 20 minutes.

4. Strain the fish stock through a sieve into a bowl and leave to cool. Portion into storage containers or bags, then freeze for up to 3 months and use as required.

Chicken stock

For this stock, it doesn't really matter whether you use raw carcasses – either from the butcher or broken down by you at home – or cooked carcasses left over from a Sunday roast.

It's the basis of so many dishes and so simple to make. So stop throwing out your chicken carcasses and stop using stock cubes! Make and freeze your stock; it's just as convenient and you'll taste the difference.

Prep time 5 minutes
Cooking time 4¼ hours
Makes 2 litres (16 cups)

~

2 chicken carcasses (see tip, above)
4 litres (16 cups) water
1 large carrot, chopped
1 large onion, chopped
2 celery sticks, chopped
1 bouquet garni (see page 272)

1. Collect the carcasses from roast chickens, or birds from which you've removed the breasts and legs. You should also be able to get these from your local butcher. Put them into a saucepan and cover with the measured water, then bring to the boil and leave to gently tick over for 10–15 minutes, skimming off all the scum with a ladle as it rises.

2. Once all the scum is removed, add your vegetables and bouquet garni and simmer, uncovered, for around 4 hours, skimming every 30 minutes or so. If the water level drops too low, add some more water. By the end of cooking, the overall liquid should have reduced by half.

3. Strain the stock through a sieve into a bowl and leave to cool. Cover, then place in the fridge overnight. Excess fat will set on top and sediment will fall to the bottom. Remove the fat and portion the stock into storage containers or bags, leaving the last bit in the bowl with the sediment (discard this). Freeze for up to 3 months and use as required.

Brown chicken stock

This takes your basic chicken stock to the next level. This is the stock you want if you are planning to use it as a broth, or for making a more profoundly flavoured sauce for a chicken dish. If you want a deep, rich chicken note in your stock, this recipe is the best version to go for. The brown colour comes from the initial roasting of the bones, which causes the Maillard reaction (see page 274).

Prep time 15 minutes
Cooking time 4½ hours
Makes 1 litre (4 cups)
~

2 chicken carcasses
500g (1¼lbs) raw chicken wings
2 celery sticks
1 large carrot
1 large onion
15g (3 fat) garlic cloves
Vegetable oil
2 litres (8 cups) water
5 thyme sprigs
2 bay leaves

1. Preheat the oven to 220°C fan (475°F). Using sturdy kitchen scissors or an old knife, you want to break down your chicken carcasses into more manageable pieces, about 5cm (2 inches) square. Place the chicken wings and carcasses on a roasting tray and roast for about 30 minutes, until golden brown.

2. Meanwhile, peel and cut the vegetables into large even pieces: a celery stick cut into 4 is about the size you're aiming for. Halve the garlic cloves. Put a large saucepan over a medium-high heat and add a little oil, then caramelise your mirepoix vegetables in the pan until nicely and evenly browned.

3. Add the roasted bones to the caramelised vegetables. Place the bone-roasting tray over a low heat and add a couple of ladles of the measured water, then bring to a simmer and scrape the tray to deglaze all the roasted chicken flavours. Pour this into the pan, along with the bones. Add the herbs and remaining water. The bones should be fully submerged; if they aren't, top up with a little more water.

4. Gently simmer the stock, uncovered, for 4 hours, skimming any froth from the surface every 30 minutes, then strain through a sieve into a bowl and leave to cool. Cover and place in the fridge overnight. The excess fat will set on top and sediment will fall to the bottom. Remove the fat and portion the stock into storage containers or bags, leaving the last bit in the bowl with all the sediment (discard this). Freeze for up to 3 months and use as required.

Beef stock

Again, it doesn't much matter if your chicken carcass here is raw or cooked, though they are easier to buy raw from a good butcher. You may anyway need to take a trip to your local butcher for the bones for this stock, as, unfortunately, I'm yet to find a supermarket that sells pig's feet. This stock is a delicious base for the best stews, pies or rich glossy sauces.

Prep time 15 minutes
Cooking time 4¾ hours
Makes 3 litres (12 cups)
~

1 chicken carcass

2kg (4½lbs) beef bones, cut into pieces (ask your butcher)

500g (1¼lbs) beef marrow bones, cut into pieces (ask your butcher)

½ pig's trotter, split vertically (ask your butcher)

2 onions

2 carrots

3 celery sticks

30g (6 fat) garlic cloves

5 litres (20 cups) water, plus more if needed

10 thyme sprigs

3 bay leaves

1. Preheat the oven to 220°C fan (475°F). Using sturdy kitchen scissors or an old knife, break down the chicken carcass into more manageable-sized pieces, about 5cm (2 inches) square. Place the beef bones, marrow bones, chicken carcass and pig's trotter on roasting trays and roast for about 30 minutes until golden brown.

2. Meanwhile, peel and cut the vegetables into large even pieces: an onion cut into 6 is about the size you're aiming for. Halve the garlic cloves. Put a large saucepan over a medium-high heat and add the fat from the bone-roasting pan, then caramelise your vegetables in the saucepan until nicely and evenly browned.

3. Add the roasted bones to the caramelised vegetables, then place the empty roasting trays over a low flame and pour in a small splash of the measured water. Bring to a simmer, scraping the trays to deglaze all the flavour, then pour the deglazing liquid into the pan, along with the bones. Add the herbs and remaining water. Your bones should be fully submerged; if they aren't, top up with a little more water.

4. Gently simmer the stock, uncovered, for 4 hours, skimming any froth from the stock every 30 minutes. Strain the stock through a sieve into a bowl and leave to cool. Cover and place in the fridge overnight. The excess fat will set on top and sediment will fall to the bottom. Remove the fat and portion the stock into storage containers or bags, leaving the last bit in the bowl with all the sediment (discard this). Freeze for up to 3 months and use as required.

Beef sauce

If you have used shop-bought stock for this, you may need to thicken your finished sauce. It's not ideal, but I always have some cornflour kicking around in my cupboards. Mix a little with water in a cup or small bowl until you have a smooth paste and add it to the sauce a teaspoon at a time, until thickened to the consistency you want.

For a glossy restaurant-quality sauce, it's important to get your stocks right. Your local butcher will be able to help you with beef trimmings for this sauce and bones for stock. This is my favourite sauce; I make a big batch and freeze it in small four-portion bags. If you want to do the same, you can easily scale up this recipe to make more at a time.

Prep time 10 minutes

Cooking time 4½ hours

Makes 500ml (2 cups)

~

250g (9oz) beef trimmings, cut into roughly 3cm (1¼ inch) pieces (ask your butcher)

100g (scant 1 cup) shallots, sliced (about 4)

25g (5 fat) garlic cloves

5g (about 5) thyme sprigs

1 bay leaf

375ml (1½ cups plus 1 tbsp) Port

375ml (1½ cups plus 1 tbsp) red wine

1 litre (4 cups) beef stock (for homemade, see page 267)

1 litre (4 cups) Brown Chicken Stock (see page 266), or good-quality shop-bought chicken stock

1. Get the largest frying pan you have for colouring the beef trim, otherwise several frying pans will do the trick. You want to make sure the beef trim is colouring in a single layer and not piled up, as this would cause it to steam and stop you from getting a nice colour. Get an even brown caramelisation on the beef.

2. Once the beef is browned off, add the shallots and garlic and colour until both are brown. Add the herbs and cook for 1 minute. Add the alcohol to the pan or pans, to deglaze all the flavour into your sauce. At this stage, if you have used multiple frying pans, you can combine everything into the same large saucepan.

3. Pour in the stocks and leave the sauce to slowly simmer, uncovered, until reduced by half. Strain the sauce through a sieve into a clean saucepan, then reduce until you have a glossy sauce.

4. Leave to cool, then cover and place in the fridge overnight. The excess fat will set on top and sediment will fall to the bottom, just as with a stock. Remove the fat and portion the sauce into storage containers or bags, leaving the last bit in the bowl with all the sediment (discard this). Freeze for up to 3 months and use as required.

How to break down poultry

HOW TO JOINT A BIRD

To cut a whole bird into 10 pieces, first firmly pull a leg away from the body. With a strong, sharp knife, or poultry shears, remove the leg at the carcass: simply cut through the skin between the leg and the body, then snap back the leg to break the thigh bone from the carcass. Cut through the joint that will have been exposed, to separate the leg from the carcass. Now break the joint between the thigh and drumstick in the same way as before, and again cut through the exposed joint. Repeat to separate and joint the other leg.

Remove the smaller 2 joints of the wing from the carcass in the same way, again breaking it at the joint first, leaving the last wing bone attached to the breast.

Now remove the breasts with those wing bones and the attached rib cage intact (strong scissors help here). Cut each across its width into 2 pieces.

Save the remaining carcass for chicken stock (see page 263). You should be left with a total of 10 pieces of chicken on the bone: 4 breast pieces, 4 leg pieces and 2 wings.

HOW TO MAKE A CROWN

Proceed as above, but do not remove the breasts from the carcass. With a sturdy sharp knife, or poultry shears, cut underneath both breasts to separate them from the rear ribs. When you hit the back bone at the base of the carcass, stop cutting. Bend the carcass back on itself to break the bones.

Now, with the knife or shears, separate the carcass from the crown, which is now ready for roasting (the carcass makes great stock).

How to cook the perfect steak

Back in the day, chefs used touch and eyeballing alone to measure when a steak was perfectly cooked. And, of course, the more experience you get in cooking steak, the better you become at that.

It's true that a steak is firmer the more cooked it becomes. However, the only way I can guarantee you perfect meat is if you use a probe thermometer and a temperature chart, but it's your call!

So here's a chart of temperatures for when you're cooking steak. Of course, you'll need a probe thermometer to measure this accurately, but you can pick those up relatively cheaply online and they're an absolute game-changer here: they take all the guesswork out of meat cookery.

You will see that there is a temperature at which you should remove the steak from the pan, then another number which is the target temperature after the meat has had a five-minute rest. Its internal temperature will continue to climb during the resting time, thanks to its own residual heat.

STEAK COOKING TEMPERATURE CHART

Rare: stop cooking at 40°C (104°F). After resting, the meat will have reached 45°C (113°F).

Medium-rare: stop cooking at 45°C (113°F). After resting, the meat will have reached 50°C (122°F).

Medium: stop cooking at 50°C (122°F). After resting, the meat will have reached 55°C (131°F).

Medium-well: stop cooking at 57°C (135°F). After resting, the meat will have reached 62°C (144°F).

Well done: stop cooking at 67°C (153°F). After resting, the meat will have reached 72°C (162°F).

Glossary

Abricoter: The glazing of pastries, tarts or fruits with a thin layer of apricot jam, to give an even, glossy finish and a touch of sweetness.

Aromats: Fragrant ingredients such as herbs and spices, used to add flavour and fragrance to recipes, most frequently when making stocks and sauces.

Bain Marie: A method used where gentle cooking is needed. A heatproof container or bowl with food is placed in or over a larger pan of hot water, allowing for an even, controlled heat. Used when melting chocolate, or baking more delicate preparations such as crème caramel.

Baveuse: A term used mainly to describe eggs, meaning slightly undercooked and with a creamy texture, particularly in omelettes. The perfect French *baveuse* omelette should be smooth, with no colour on the outside and a centre that is soft and somewhat runny.

Beurre Manié: A thickening agent similar to a roux. It's made by mixing equal parts of softened butter and flour together, which is rolled into small balls and dropped into soups or sauces towards the end of cooking to both thicken them and to add richness.

Beurre Noisette: We call this 'brown butter' in England. It's butter that is cooked until it has a golden-brown colour and a nutty aroma. Mixed with a little lemon juice, it makes the perfect sauce to go with fish.

Blanch: This term is usually used for vegetables, but you can blanch anything. It's the process of briefly putting something in boiling water and then straight into iced water to stop the cooking. This technique is used to preserve colour, quickly cook, or to help remove skins (from tomatoes, say, or peaches).

Bouquet Garni: A small bundle of herbs and herb stalks, usually hard herbs including bay leaf, thyme and parsley, tied together with kitchen string. Used in stocks, sauces and stews to add flavour and easily removed by means of the string.

Brunoise: A precise knife-cut in which vegetables are cut into small, even 5mm (⅛-inch) dice.

Cartouche: A round piece of baking paper, often with a small hole in the centre, placed directly on the surface of a simmering liquid or food to slow down evaporation and prevent a skin from forming. It's the happy medium between uncovered and covered.

Chiffonade: Another knife-cut technique, mainly used to slice leafy vegetables, herbs or salad leaves into long, thin ribbons. The leaves are usually stacked, rolled, then sliced, creating fine strips.

Clarified: A process in which butter or liquids are treated to remove all impurities and are left completely clear. Butter is melted and the water content and milk solids are removed, leaving behind pure butterfat. Another clarifying method is when cloudy stocks are cooked with egg whites, which capture fats and impurities in a solid floating layer, leaving the remaining liquid underneath completely clear.

Confit: A traditional method of cooking and preserving food, usually meat (see page 160 for a recipe for confit duck). It's first salted and then cooked in its own fat at a low temperature for an extended period. The food, once cooked, is often stored in the fat to preserve it.

Cuisson: Translates to 'cooking' in English, but in French refers to the doneness of meats. Rare, medium and well-done are all different kinds of *cuisson.*

Deglaze: A technique in which a liquid, usually wine, stock or vinegar, is added to a hot pan after searing meat or vegetables. The liquid helps dissolve the caramelised bits stuck to the pan, so no flavour is lost.

En Papillote: A cooking method used for fish or vegetables, in which food is sealed in a baking paper or foil pouch, then baked. The steam trapped inside the pouch cooks the food, but keeps it moist at the same time.

Flambé: When liquor with a high alcohol content (often brandy) is added to a hot pan and then ignited with a long-handled match or by tipping the pan away from you towards the flame, creating a burst of flames. Used to quickly burn off the alcohol in cooking, but also as a way of creating tableside theatre in a restaurant when cooking dishes such as steak Diane.

Gratinate: To cook a dish, usually under a hot grill, until the surface is golden brown and crispy. Or, in pastry terms, to sprinkle with sugar and blowtorch until caramelised and crisp.

Grenobloise: A classic French preparation very similar to *meunière*, in which, as well as the usual browned butter, lemon and parsley, there is also the addition of capers, croutons and sometimes other shellfish such as brown shrimps.

Julienne: A knife-cut technique in which vegetables are cut into small matchsticks, around 5cm (2 inches) in length and 2–5mm ($\frac{1}{12}$–$\frac{1}{4}$ inch) along the sides.

Jus: A fancy French gravy or sauce.

Lardons: The word used to describe bacon that has been cut into small strips, around 3cm (1¼ inches) in length and 1cm (½ inch) along the sides. They're often rendered until crisp and used in salads, stews and other dishes, such as quiche Lorraine.

Macerate: Often used in desserts, this is when fruits are soaked in syrups or alcohol – or tomatoes in salad dressings – to soften them and infuse them with flavour.

Maillard Reaction: To get scientific, this is a chemical reaction between amino acids and reducing sugars that occurs when food is browned in a hot pan, giving it flavour and colour. This reaction is fundamental in the cooking of meats, breads and many other foods. The browning process only happens at high temperatures and is what gives meat its rich, savoury flavours.

Mandolin: A piece of equipment used for slicing foods very thinly and evenly. It typically has an adjustable blade to change the thickness of slices. Great for Dauphinois, or other recipes that require a lot of slicing.

Medallions: Small slices of meat, usually cut from the fillet or loin. Medallions can be seared and served as individual portions, or flattened for Cordon Bleu (see page 145).

Mirepoix: The foundational mix of vegetables, usually onions, carrots and celery. Used to add flavour in stocks, stews and sauces.

Mother Sauces: The five foundational sauces in French cuisine from which many other sauces are made: Béchamel, Espagnole, Hollandaise, Tomato and Velouté are the five basic sauces every cook should learn how to make.

Oeuf: French for 'egg', you may know this one and, if the chapter full of egg dishes wasn't a big enough clue, I thought I'd leave it here just to make sure.

Pané: The process of coating food with flour, lightly beaten egg and breadcrumbs before frying.

Render: Used to describe the slow cooking of fat until it melts and separates from the solid parts of meat. The rendered fat can be collected and used for cooking, leaving a thin, crisp, caramelised layer of fat on the meat you are cooking.

Ribbon Stage: A term used in baking to describe eggs and sugar that have been beaten until thick and pale: when the whisk is lifted, the batter should fall in a ribbon-like trail that briefly sits on the surface of the mixture before sinking.

Roux: A mixture of equal parts of flour and fat (usually butter), cooked together and used as a thickening agent for sauces, soups and stews. Roux can be white, blonde or brown, depending on the cooking time. The opposite of *beurre manié* (see previous page), which is added to a finished sauce to thicken, a roux is used at the start and thin liquid is added to it. The most famous sauce which uses a roux is one of the mother sauces: Béchamel (see page 255).

Sauté: A cooking method in which food is cooked in a small amount of fat over a fairly high heat. The food is tossed or stirred frequently to cook it evenly and develop a slight browning without steaming.

Sear: A technique in which food is cooked at a high temperature to create a caramelised crust on the outside. Searing is often the first step before finishing cooking by roasting or braising.

Sweat: A gentle cooking method in which vegetables are cooked in a small amount of fat over a low heat, sometimes covered, to soften them and release their moisture without browning.

Tamis: A drum-shaped, fine-meshed sieve used to achieve an ultra-smooth texture. It's often used to purée food, most commonly potatoes.

Trivet: Placed inside a roasting pan to lift food above the drippings and allow heat to evenly circulate. A trivet can be a piece of metal, or a mixture of vegetables: carrots and onions are the most popular.

Velouté: One of the five French mother sauces (see opposite), as with béchamel it starts with a roux (see above), but instead of milk, the liquid used is a light stock of fish or meat. Velouté serves as a base for many sauces and is known for its smooth, velvety texture.

Index

S

salads
 carottes râpées 32
 chicory salad, capers,
  parsley 196
 green salad 197
 radicchio, walnut, pear,
  Roquefort 201
 salade niçoise 40
 tomato salad, *vierge*
  dressing 208
salmon
 salmon en croûte 120–1
 salmon *rillettes* 43
salt-baked sea bass 112–13
sauce gribiche, green asparagus
 209
sauce pistou, ratatouille, 193
sauce ravigote, globe artichoke
 202–3
sauces
 béchamel sauce 255
 beef sauce 269
 le grand aïoli 21
 hollandaise sauce 259
 mornay sauce 255
scallops: *coquilles Saint Jacques*
 90–1
sea bass, salt-baked 112–13
shallots
 nage 260
 pommes rösti 185
shellfish cocktail 44
 see also types of shellfish
shrimps: *sole meunière* 116–17
smoked salmon *rillettes* 43
sole meunière 116–17
soufflés
 raspberry soufflés 224–5
 twice-cooked cheese
  soufflés 78–9
soups
 bouillabaisse with rouille
  96–7
 French onion soup 22
 soupe au pistou 26
 vichyssoise 36

spinach: salmon en croûte
 120–1
spring cabbage, anchoïade,
 chilli 212
spring onions: salade niçoise
 40
starters 18–57
steak
 cooking the perfect steak
  271
 steak au poivre 133
 steak Diane 152
stews
 beef bourguignon 154–5
 coq au vin 148–9
 lamb navarin 146
 poulet basquaise 165
stock
 beef stock 267
 brown chicken stock 266
 chicken stock 263
 fish stock 262
 nage 260
sunflower seeds: dukkah 32

T

tartare, beef 53
tartiflette 175
tarts
 apple *tarte fine* 218–19
 tarte Tatin 246
terrine, country 54–5
tomato ketchup: shellfish
 cocktail 44
tomatoes
 beef tartare 53
 bouillabaisse with rouille
  96–7
 chicken chasseur 138
 hake with Provençal sauce
  101
 oeufs piperade 65
 poulet basquaise 165
 ratatouille, *sauce pistou* 193
 salade niçoise 40
 tomato salad, *vierge*
  dressing 208

tomme fraîche: pommes aligot
 171
tuna: salade niçoise 40
turnips: lamb navarin 146
twice-cooked cheese soufflés
 78–9

V

veal cordon bleu 145
vegetables
 le grand aïoli 21
 see also types of vegetable
velouté, fish 102–3
vichyssoise 36
vierge dressing, tomato salad
 208
vinaigrette 253
 leeks vinaigrette 190

W

walnuts: radicchio, walnut,
 pear, Roquefort 201
wild mushrooms: pork chop,
 braised butter beans 159
wine
 beef bourguignon 154–5
 beef sauce 269
 cod with pea fricassée 86
 coq au vin 148–9
 French onion soup 22
 globe artichoke, *sauce
  ravigote* 202–3
 moules marinière 111
 nage 260
 pork chop, braised butter
  beans 159

Menu

- Coq Au Riesling Pie
- Chicken Cordon Bley
- Spatchcock + Chips
- Coq Au Vin
- Chicken Kiev
- Chicken Chasseur
- Vadouvan Chicken Curry
- Garlic Chicken
- Poulet Basquaise

#Chicken Classics

Acknowledgements

Creating *French Classics* has been an extraordinary journey, one I could never have accomplished alone. This book is as much a reflection of the incredible people in my life as it is my love for French cuisine. As it's a book of the greatest hits of French food, I suppose I should tip my hat to the peasants who cooked what they had to hand, the farmers, fisherman and chefs across France who made all of these wonderful dishes the classics they are today.

To my wife, Rachel, and our beautiful son Alfie, you are my inspiration and anchor, your unwavering love and belief in me have been my constant source of courage and motivation. Thank you for being by my side through every step of this project, and my entire career for that matter; you are a saint for putting up with me.

I want to express my heartfelt gratitude to my parents. You instilled in me the values of integrity, kindness and perseverance, alongside a strong work ethic. These have guided me on my journey and have been instrumental in bringing me to this point. To my wider family and friends, thank you for endless encouragement and for being there in so many ways, big and small, throughout my life. I'm forever grateful for your love and support. Brad, thanks for your help getting this one over the line.

To everyone at Maison François and Café François, thank you. François O'Neill, Ed Wyand and João Figueiredo (who rocks the kitchen like no other). Working with like-minded, passionate people is a joy. Over the past five years we've created something very special which I'm immensely proud of. You've helped shape not just this book, but so much of what I love about our work together.

To all the chefs and mentors, too many to mention, you have all moulded me into the chef I am today. My college lecturer David Boland, you sparked my love for French cuisine and instilled in me the skills and discipline that have brought me here. I owe so much to your guidance and inspiration.

My incredible book agent, Emily Sweet, thank you for believing in *French Classics* and for guiding me through every step of the process. Your support has been invaluable.

To the publishing team at Bloomsbury. Rowan Yapp, Kiron Gill and my brilliant editor Lucy Bannell and designer Louise Brigenshaw, thank you for your insights, hard work and dedication. You have helped bring this vision to life in ways I couldn't have imagined; working with such a well-respected publishing house has been very special. A group of very talented people gave this book its soul: Patricia Niven, Sam Reeves, Valerie Berry, Eden Owen-Jones and Rachel Vere, your artistry have brought the heart of *French Classics* to every page. And to Daniel Illsley, whose stunning illustrations elevate this book to a new level, your talent is unparalleled.

It was social media that really kicked off this book journey. So, Thomas Straker, you kindly let me use your studio and gave me the tools to get the wheels in motion; thank you also for your introduction to Mandy, whose editing in this social media whirlwind has helped this book find its audience in the most exciting way.

And finally, to you, the readers, thank you for letting me share my passion for French cuisine with you. It's an honour to have *French Classics* become part of your culinary journey. I hope this book inspires you to explore, create and enjoy the magic of French cooking. With love, *à bientôt*.

About the author

Matthew Ryle is a British chef whose heart is in French food. He was brought up in a village called Purley on Thames, near Reading. Aged 15, Matt began his culinary journey in the Michelin-starred kitchen of L'Ortolan restaurant in Reading, before, as a food-fixated teenager, he flew the nest in the pursuit of food. It was in a French-focused chef school where Matt discovered the fundamentals which laid the foundations for his career. While exploring the history and traditions of French cuisine and cooking classic dishes, his passion for the country's food was truly ignited.

After years in top London kitchens, in 2018 Matt competed on *MasterChef: The Professionals*, in which he won the runner-up position. In 2020, Matt launched French brasserie Maison François, earning critical acclaim and multiple awards. Building on its success, he opened Café François in 2024. Alongside the two busy, bustling brasseries in central London, Matt has built a large social media audience of more than 2.5 million, with whom he shares his classic French recipes.

BLOOMSBURY PUBLISHING

Bloomsbury Publishing Inc.

1359 Broadway, New York, NY 10018, USA

50 Bedford Square, London, WC1B 3DP, UK

Bloomsbury Publishing Ireland Limited, 29 Earlsfort Terrace, Dublin 2, D02 AY28, Ireland

BLOOMSBURY, BLOOMSBURY PUBLISHING and the Diana logo are trademarks of Bloomsbury Publishing Plc

First published in Great Britain in 2025

First published in the United States by Bloomsbury Publishing in 2025

Text © Matthew Ryle, 2025

Photographs © Patricia Niven, 2025

The publisher would like to thank the Photobook Café for the loan of the chair used on pages 63, 70, 83 and 153.

Library of Congress Cataloging-in-Publication Data is available.

ISBN: HB: 978-1-63973-684-3; eBook: 978-1-63973-685-0

2 4 6 8 10 9 7 5 3 1

Editor: Lucy Bannell

Designer: Louise Brigenshaw

Photographer: Patricia Niven

Photographer's Assistant: Sam Reeves

Food Stylist: Valerie Berry

Prop Stylist: Rachel Vere

Illustrator: Daniel Illsley

Printed and bound in China by Toppan Leefung Printing Ltd

To find out more about our authors and books visit **www.bloomsbury.com** and sign up for our newsletters. Bloomsbury books may be purchased for business or promotional use. For information on bulk purchases please contact Macmillan Corporate and Premium Sales Department at specialmarkets@macmillan.com. For product safety-related questions contact productsafety@bloomsbury.com.

RECIPE NOTES

All butter should be unsalted, unless stated otherwise.

I've occasionally mentioned pancetta (which is Italian, not French) in this book. This is because, at my restaurants, we use pancetta ventreche, which is French, but is hard to come by. Any salted, smoked, cured belly bacon will be fine.

US RECIPE NOTES

Please note that the recipes on pages 21, 40, 53, 58–83, 96–97, 201, 216, 242 and 253 contain raw or lightly cooked egg and, in the US, are not recommended for people with a compromised immune system, the elderly or the very young.

Cup and tablespoon measures are for the prepared ingredient (such as grated, finely chopped and so on).

For whipping cream, substitute heavy cream.

Although ingredients are given in metric and US cups, please only use one set of measurements.

Flour, sugar and salt cup measurements are spooned and leveled.

All other measurements are loosely packed, unless stated otherwise.

UK:US GLOSSARY OF TERMS

aubergine – eggplant

baby onions – pearl onions

beef dripping – beef tallow

brown shrimps – salad shrimps

caster sugar – superfine sugar

celeriac – celery root

chicory – Belgian endive

chips – french fries

cornflour – cornstarch

courgettes – zucchini

cucumber – English cucumber

Demerara sugar – turbinado sugar

double cream – heavy cream

fillet steak – filet mignon

flaked almonds – sliced almonds

ground almonds – almond flour

icing sugar – confectioners' sugar

plain flour – all-purpose flour

prawns – shrimp

pudding rice – risotto rice

sirloin steak – strip steak

spring cabbage – pointed cabbage

tomato purée – tomato paste